BREAKING FREE
from
RELIGIOUS OPPRESSION

SIDDIQAH VERRETT

Copyright © 2014 by Siddiqah Verrett

Breaking Free from Religious Oppression
by Siddiqah Verrett

Printed in the United States of America

ISBN 9781629526324

All rights reserved solely by the author. The author guarantees all contents are original and do not infringe upon the legal rights of any other person or work. No part of this book may be reproduced in any form without the permission of the author. The views expressed in this book are not necessarily those of the publisher.

Scripture quotations taken from the New International Version (NIV). Copyright © 1973, 1978, 1984, 2011 by Biblica, Inc.™. Used by permission. All rights reserved.

www.xulonpress.com

Dedication

I dedicate this book to my husband, Derek Verrett, who stood by me through thick and thin; my mother, Aisha Frey, who prayed for us; my father, Abdul Ali, who always supported us; Bishop Shawn D. Smith and Elder Tammy Smith for leading us on the path toward God's love; Pastor Timothy Jones and Pastors Joseph and Carolyn Tumpkin for praying for us and letting God's healing waters flow in our lives while we sat under their ministry.

Special thanks to my friends Marcy Moore and Demetria Wilson, whom the Lord brought into my life to walk with me in the midst of these tremendous hardships and overwhelming challenges.

Introduction

I am a married mother of two daughters who were infants at the time of these events, and I want to share how I went from being stuck in "religion" to breaking free and having relationship with God. This book depicts my personal journey of breaking free from the religious world of control and manipulation driven by abusive, false-teaching leadership. This book is designed to bring healing to those who have had similar experiences and to break the fetters of religion, legalism (strict adherence to the letter of the law), pride, and condemnation (criticism) placed on people who love God wholeheartedly but feel compelled by religious works to prove themselves to God in order to receive his love.

I intend to reveal Christ's love for all humanity and unveil the grace of God through faith. Through my personal experiences, I will uncover the very real powers that operate in the church. I want you to experience the fullness of salvation and the freedom Christ has given us by way of the cross. My book discloses how spiritual leaders manipulated us, took over our lives, and destroyed our finances, costing me my military career, my credit score, my home, and my car, and left my family financially stripped and emotionally wounded.

God has enabled me to share my story in order to bring redemption to others. This book is by no means intended to attack any religious organization but to encourage the hearts of the broken, break the chains of the spiritually bound, and hinder the assignment of the religious oppressor by faith.

I consider my book the Underground Railroad to freedom in Christ. As you may know, the actual Underground Railroad was not a railroad built underground but escape routes that led slaves toward freedom. It was a system of hidden routes, transportation, and safe houses that led black slaves to their freedom with the help of abolitionists who stood firmly against enslavement. Well, call me an abolitionist against religious oppression. My intent is to assist in the process of leading others to freedom and to reveal God's *love* for all humanity.

No more shall we as believers in Christ suffer at the hands of demonic pseudo-psychology that has crept onto God's threshing floor by way of ill-intentioned wolves in sheep's' clothing. As a body, we shall overcome the sinister ambush of the enemy disguising himself as light to distract and replace our God-given faith with false condemnations, distrust, and betrayal that ultimately subdue our lives for his own purposes.

I beseech you to reexamine your spiritual authenticity, analyze your finances against your heart's desire to fulfill the kingdom, and see how your "checkbook" balances. All too often we replace our faith with pecuniary gifts as if the answer is to give it away rather than to pray, fast, and seek God's face to destroy the yoke. Our empowerment is in the hands of the Holy Spirit, and if we find ourselves buying those gifts, we are *dead wrong*.

This is my story of how the Lord brought my family out of religion—stage-managed religion—and into relationship with Him. It is my journey of being enslaved by religious control and manipulation by works of righteousness, condemnation, and reproach and how the Lord enabled me to enter into His loving kindness through His redeeming power. This book is a spiritual guide toward freedom. Think of it as a safe house on the route to freedom. You may enter into the Father's rest.

Contents

1. My Journey Begins......................9
2. Moving On...........................16
3. Behavior Control......................25
4. Emotional Control....................33
5. Fellowship in His Suffering..............43
6. The Enslaved Mind-Set.................51
7. Coming Out..........................56
8. Ownership 70
9. Religion.............................74
10. Relationship 82

Chapter 1

My Journey Begins

Over the years I have had some awesome experiences in my journey of living for Jesus. I accepted Him into my heart as a little girl, so I knew of His existence, but I didn't fully understand what it was to have a personal relationship with Him. My mom was a devout Muslim-turned-Christian. She introduced me to Christ as a child, and I watched her connection with God grow and develop into a beautiful relationship. She spent countless hours in prayer: crying, singing, and worshipping Him.

I sensed she had something special, though I wasn't sure what exactly, and I believed in God because she did. She took us to church faithfully, which made me feel like I knew God, too, even though I knew Him only through her view of him. My mom invested in teaching my two sisters and me the Christian way, posting Scriptures on our bedroom walls for memorization and reading Bible-based stories to us at night.

My dad remained a devout Muslim. Oftentimes in the morning I would watch him laying out his *sajada*, a small embroidered prayer rug, and bow down saying a repetitious prayer. He prayed more quietly and in a more controlled way than my mother. I was intrigued and fascinated by this, since I wasn't really much of a crier. I was interested in his quiet Arabic chants and song, and I thought it was awesome to be disciplined in prayer like him.

At the age of nineteen, I left home and joined the military. My first duty station was Misawa Air Base, Japan, and it was there that I truly found God for myself. At first I'd lived my life the way I wanted to, trying to find myself without the Lord's help. I believed that God knew me because I pretty much grew up in the church, but little did I know that I was outside of relationship with him. For several months, a co-worker invited me to church until I finally said yes. So I went to Greater Love Missionary Baptist Church one Sunday morning.

During the service, the congregation joyfully praised the Lord, and before I knew it I was clapping and praising the Lord, too. People sang, jumped, and shouted, and it appeared as if they were being set free, healed, and delivered. I longed for what they had. I wanted to feel the things they felt.

My life felt empty. I seemed to be lacking something. There was no fulfillment. I felt pleasure at times, but still void. I needed something to fill that emptiness. I needed Jesus for myself—not because anybody else said I did but because I needed to have an experience with God. I told my husband, Derek, about the little Baptist church I had visited, and he decided to go with me on Easter Sunday.

We were inspired by the word and left encouraged, feeling a sense of fulfillment and joy. So we went to the church again for Wednesday-night Bible study. The senior pastor presented a message on salvation, and there was no denying the Lord's presence in the church. The fire of God was so strong that it consumed every dead thing inside me. For once, I felt alive! My husband felt it, too. He grabbed my hand tightly and whispered in my ear, "Let's go to the altar."

Before I could answer him, he was pulling me up there with him. I couldn't resist the nudging of the Lord in my own heart anyway, so I went willingly. Once I got there, I couldn't help but weep before the Lord, and my husband stood with tears in his eyes.

I remember the pastor asking if we wanted to receive Jesus as our personal Lord and savior.

We both replied, "Yes." We then prayed a prayer of confession and the prayer of salvation and received Jesus in our hearts. Instantly I felt brand new.

Shame had left me, guilt had left me, sadness had left me, and I felt a joy like no other. It was as if I could see more clearly—all the cloudiness was swept away. It was a feeling of being set free, sober, and awakened. I felt that all of God's focus was on me in that moment and that He cared so much for me because He knew who I was. It was truly remarkable.

I've got Jesus now!

My relationship with Christ continued to grow after that. In my prayer time, He gave me revelation after revelation. He would open my eyes to the word and give me understanding. He made me feel special, and all I wanted to do was bask in His presence. I sang to Him, I danced before Him, and He shared His love with me.

"I want to do more for you, God!" I cried out one morning. "I want to do something big in the kingdom! I want to operate in ministry the way Darlene Bishop and Juanita Bynum does. I want to preach hard and sweat through my hair and not care because I'm serious about you! I want to experience church mothers' laying hands and tarrying until Jesus comes. I want a righteous indignation where foolishness is not tolerated. Give me all that you have for me, God!"

He gave me what I asked for.

I was stationed in Japan for four years, and my relationship with the Lord grew stronger and stronger. I felt as if He were calling me to leadership, so I began to minister the word to whomever I came into contact with. I wanted to see souls saved from destructive lifestyles and people healed, delivered, and set free from bondage.

I prayed with women at my workplace, I invited them into my home, and I went to theirs when they sought healing and prayer. I didn't know what I was doing—the Holy Spirit led me every time.

I remember one particular woman who called me at home.

"Can you and Minister Mary pray with me?" she said, crying. "I need prayer right now. I am under spiritual attack." I could hear the desperation in her voice.

"Sure. Let me call Mary to see if she's available."

She was, and we all agreed to meet at Mary's house.

The woman arrived looking almost sick. "Please help me," she said. "I need prayer."

We asked what was going on.

"Before I came to know the Lord, I was in a cult. I did things I should not have done back home in Florida, and I participated in secret matters of the demonic, and now they are in my house!"

"What do you mean they are in your house?" I said. "You got saved years ago, and now you're located in Japan."

"My cult members have astral-projected into my home and now they are tormenting me!"

I felt my eyes widen. *Oh, this is not for me. I'm sure Minister Mary knows what to do.* Minister Mary was much older than I was, and I looked up to her because she had so much wisdom and knowledge. She knew the word of God.

When we began to pray for her, the woman got on her knees in desperation. "Help me! Help me!" she cried and knelt in front of Minister Mary. "Help me."

I felt the Holy Spirit come and rest on me, and I started speaking in tongues uncontrollably. The Lord instructed me to place my hands above the woman's head without touching her, just moving my hands back and forth from the front of her forehead to the back of her head.

The thought of this scared me. I didn't understand why He didn't instruct Minister Mary to do this—the woman was right in front of her. The more I questioned the Lord about it, the harder He pushed me to do it. My heart raced.

My tongues grew louder as I tried to resist the urgency of the spirit, though I knew I had to be obedient and do what God said to do.

Suddenly, Minister Mary looked at me. "Dee, do what the Lord has instructed *you* to do," she said.

I got onto my knees and faced the woman and did exactly what the Lord instructed. I was nervous and scared, but to my surprise the woman got up off the floor and shouted, "Ahhhh! They are gone, I'm free, I'm free, and they are gone!" Then she laughed.

I was in utter shock. It was over. The woman had been set free and all was well, just like that. We thanked the Lord for her freedom, and I quickly drove home.

What was that about? I had never experienced anything like that in my life. Why did God use me?

After that experience, my husband and I started to attend leadership training classes at our church. I felt as if I'd been called to do something in the kingdom, but I didn't know exactly what. Leadership classes gave us a new perspective on the word of God. We learned about the Hebrew and Greek translations of Scripture, which helped us to understand the context of Scripture a little better. We were faithful and dedicated to the ministry, spending most of our time helping the ministry reach others through Christ however we could.

During this time, my oldest daughter, Maliya, was born. At 7 pounds 11 ounces, she was the most beautiful thing I'd ever laid eyes on. I wanted to be the best mother I could be to her, but I was clueless about caring for a baby. As it turned out, our Greater Love church family came to my aid and became our family. They supported us every step of the way, donating baby clothes, cribs, strollers, walkers, and even going as far as cooking meals for us for two weeks after my delivery. They embraced us with the love of Christ and gave us room to grow and develop as new parents. We gathered together for potlucks, prayer, movie nights, worship services, you name it. We went on retreats and conferences throughout Japan and fellowshipped with other local Christian ministries.

During one of our training classes, an unexpected thing happened. The pastor announced to the class that the Lord placed it in his heart to have my husband preach a sermon because he wanted him to become licensed for ministry before we PCS'd (permanent change of station) to Colorado. I chuckled at the thought.

"I don't know why you laugh," Pastor Smith said, "because you will follow behind your husband with your initial sermon as well, so be prepared."

I couldn't believe it. We were moving to Colorado in less than two weeks! How was I supposed to prepare? I'm not a public speaker. I get nervous and feel faint in crowds. I couldn't possibly stand before a crowd and preach a sermon. I didn't have the skill.

"I have set the date for two days before you leave Japan," the pastor said. "The Lord told me that you will need your license for ministry purposes in the United States."

My husband and I traded worried looks, but we accepted it as a message from the Lord—even though we felt by no means ready for this.

As the sermon date neared, panic and fear grew within me. I cried day and night—literally. "Lord, I've got nothing," I would say to Him. "I don't know where to start. I don't know how to speak. I can't articulate words like a preacher. I'm still a baby. How did I get here? Please don't do this to me."

When the pastor invited us to his home for dinner to discuss our progress on the sermons, I looked at it as an opportunity to let him know that I couldn't do the sermon. I tried to hold back the tears as I explained to him that I just didn't have it in me to preach.

He smiled at me. "You'll be fine. What passage of Scripture has the Lord placed in your heart?"

I told him I'd been looking at 1 Corinthians 13, the Scriptures on love. He looked at me with a big smile and told me that that had been his initial sermon topic years ago.

My Journey Begins

We shared a laugh. I couldn't believe I'd picked the same one. For some reason, hearing that made me more anxious about the whole thing, and I later asked the Lord what he would like me to say, and to my surprise he gave me a message!

When the day came to stand before God's people and deliver the message, I was gripped by fear and anxiety. Before the evening service, my husband and I were called into the pastor's office to prepare for our message. When we got there, my eyes quickly filled with tears and I cried a hard ugly cry, begging the pastor not to let me go out there.

He looked at me and patted my back. "You'll be all right ... You'll be all right."

I could hear the worship music coming to an end and knew my time was right around the corner. I shook with fear. The worship team walked off the platform and into the pastor's office, and the worship leader approached me. "What's wrong, baby?"

I looked up at her with my ugly crying face. "I can't ... I don't want to do this." Gasping, I could barely get the words out.

She grabbed my hands and prayed with me a prayer of faith, encouraging my heart to allow the Lord to use me. Afterward, I clutched my Bible and my notes, took a deep breath, and proceeded to the sanctuary. I stood before the people and spoke from my spirit of the things that the Lord had told me while I studied in my prayer time. I spoke of the love of God, and I found that His spirit enabled me to address the passages of Scripture I had studied with clarity, boldness, and conviction. Before I knew it, people were crying and hugging, blessed by the word.

God had shown up for me and for them, and I received my minister's license from Greater Love Missionary Baptist Church. Quite frankly, though, the thought of being a minister terrified me.

What will be required of me?

Chapter 2

Moving On

Colorado Springs was like a breath of fresh, cold, crisp air. The scenery was beyond pleasurable, the atmosphere was great, the people seemed to be friendly, and we always had a perfect view of Pikes Peak and the surrounding snowcapped mountains. I remember thinking to myself, "I can't wait to experience God here. What church are we going to go to, and how soon will we find it?"

We visited several churches, and I distinctly recall the one whose services aired on the Trinity Broadcasting Network (TBN) from time to time and where, at the end of service, an elder came down from the platform and approached my husband and me and said he had a prophetic word from the Lord that he wanted to share with us.

"Your family is going to go through a financial crisis," he said, "and the enemy is going to have your wife backed into a corner. When I look at her, I see her with her hands on her face crying, but the Lord is going to deliver you out of it."

I was bewildered. The devil is a liar. Why is he telling us this? We weren't struggling financially! In fact, we were doing great financially. Derek had a new job working at Family Christian

Bookstore, and I was continuing my military career. We thanked him for telling us and left the church scratching our heads.

After several months, we were still without a church home. We continued to visit churches, but none of them were anything like what we were used to. We were ministers, and we wanted to get plugged into a ministry that would use us and help us develop as ministers. Then one day a customer at the bookstore invited my husband to a church and handed him a business card with a picture of a pastor and his wife on the front.

"What do you think about going to Bible study tonight?" Derek said when he came home.

Exhausted after a long day, I pulled off one of my military boots. The thought of visiting another church in the next two hours didn't appeal to me. But when I closely examined the pastors' smiling faces on the card, I figured why not? We could give it a try. After making a quick bite to eat, we headed out.

We had a hard time finding the church until we saw its name on a white sign with burgundy letters posted on the back wall of what appeared to be a huge storage facility. When we walked in, worship was already in session, so we quietly found some seats.

It took no time to enter into the presence of the Lord. Almost instantly, I felt a connection with the flow of worship. It felt pure and true. And the worship team sang with intensity and heartfelt emotion that words couldn't explain. The service was mind-blowing.

After the worship, Pastor George began a Bible study lesson. We sat quietly listening until we heard the back doors of the church open and then close. Everyone turned to see a tall dark-skinned woman wearing a lime-green blouse and white designer pants. With her head held high, she walked to the front row and sat down. An odd silence lurked in the room.

"Good evening, sweetie. How are you?" Pastor George said slowly as the woman sat down.

She nodded for him to proceed, saying she was well.

I put two and two together and figured out that she was the woman on the card Derek had brought home—the pastor's wife—but for some reason she looked very different in person. A little more stern and serious.

Immediately after the service, the woman approached me and began to prophesy about my life. She mentioned a personal prayer I'd prayed before coming to Colorado and said the Lord was answering my prayers right now!

I didn't know this woman from Adam! How did she know my prayer?

Everyone gathered around us and stared in astonishment as she laid hands on me and said she could feel God's anointing. Before I knew it, I was lying on the floor weeping before the Lord. I couldn't believe it. Everything she'd said was true.

Afterward, my husband and I knew this was where we were supposed to be.

We joined the church the following Sunday. We were excited to worship with the congregation again and walked into the building with huge smiles on our faces, thinking about what had taken place there a few days before. We felt like this was our new family, and somehow we just fit right in.

After we sat, I lifted my head to see three teenage girls sitting in the last row, and to my surprise they stared at me with a look of utter hatred. I smiled and said, "Hello," and they glared at me from head to toe as if I were some sort of threat to them.

I later found out that they were three of the pastor's seven daughters.

Joining the church

Our new church family was amazing. The members quoted Scripture at the drop of a hat. It just seemed to flow out. They seemed to be very skilled and mature and well-equipped when it came to maneuvering that sword known as the word. They had church mothers, nurses with the hats, armor bearers, and security! *This is it. The church I asked God for!*

The teachings were so rich, the anointing was so thick, I couldn't explain what I was feeling. I yearned to be on the same level as this ministry. The worship pulled me in every time, I felt so connected. These were my kind of people—they had no problem lingering in worship until the Holy Spirit showed up. I was truly awestruck and couldn't understand why the services weren't packed. There were only ten to twenty regular members, but I didn't care. I was where I was supposed to be.

These people had an ability to decipher and interpret doctrines and philosophies in a way I had never heard before. Their knowledge challenged everything I believed to be true. The pastors preached with great conviction, and all I could do after every service was weep and say, "Wow, that word was rich." However, I started to doubt that I was truly saved and destined to go to heaven. I began to feel unworthy and inadequate, as if I weren't good enough for God and He expected more from me. Condemnation came to be the predominant feeling within my soul after the services. It was a deep overwhelming sadness that seemed to come from disapproval and reproach. All I knew was that I wanted to be better than what I was and that I would do whatever it took to be a servant of God.

Shepherd's Call

We were required to attend Shepherd's Call, a monthly Sunday-evening prayer service during which the church members prayed for an hour. I didn't know what to expect but thought it would be something great. When we arrived, we were handed white sheets to wrap ourselves in and given olive oil to anoint our hands with. We then followed the others as they circled the sanctuary, walking and praying quietly.

The sanctuary was dark, but there were three lights shining from the pulpit. We continued to circle for about thirty minutes, and then one of the elders got on the microphone to pray. Everyone proceeded toward the altar together to continue to pray. My husband and I watched as the others either got onto their knees or lay flat on their bellies. We didn't know what was going on until we heard the prayer leader shout for the people to travail. I didn't know what travailing was, so I just sat tensely and watched.

Everyone was shouting, crying, moaning, screaming, and wailing in front of the altar. Derek and I got on our knees and hid under the white sheets, both unnerved. I knelt close to him, waiting to follow his lead, and then I heard Dr. Sharon approach us. She placed one hand on my back and one on my belly and whispered sharply, "Out of your belly!" I realized that this meant to wail or holler boisterously, so I let out an embarrassing flutter of a moan but soon got the hang of it. Then she did the same with Derek, pushing him to shout.

In the months afterward, I was often laid out on the altar weeping and sobbing for God to make me a pure vessel. I remember one particular Shepherd's Call that came when I was on my knees crying out to the Lord with my arms outstretched. Dr. Sharon approached me in a spiritual rant and aggressively pushed the palms of her hands into my belly. "*You belong to me!*" she shouted.

I doubled over from the blow and lay there trembling under the power of what had just taken place. I was in awe, not pain. I had never seen her do this to anyone before. I was astonished that she'd taken interest in me this way. And I *wanted* to belong to her.

I embraced her doctrine as "the truth" because she spoke so aggressively. I desired all that God had for me; I wanted to live in His presence.

The pastors were pretty intense, continually pushing us to pray more, fast more, and travail harder. They demanded that we follow and stay in covenant with their ministry—and their ministry only—because they knew the truth about godly living. All other churches were considered weak and undisciplined. They declared that they had their fingers on the pulse of God and knew exactly what He wanted for our lives.

One Sunday after church, Dr. Sharon asked me to sit down with her because she desperately needed to share something important with me. She went on to express that the Lord had sent me to her to minister to her just as Elisha ministered to Elijah in Scripture (1 Kings 19:21). She said she'd known it the moment she laid hands on me. "You must stay on my heels, you hear me?" she said. "God has chosen you to receive an impartation of my anointing."

She articulated how Elisha ate, dressed, looked, and spoke like the prophet Elijah and how I must take heed and do the same thing because of the prophetic call on my life.

This intrigued me and I wanted to know more. She told me that committing one's life to another in order to receive her anointing was biblical, based on 1 Kings 19:20-21:

> "Elisha then left his oxen and ran after Elijah. 'Let me kiss my father and mother goodbye,' he said, 'and then I will come with you.'
> 'Go back,' Elijah replied. 'What have I done to you?' "

I respected her and trusted that she had my best interests at heart, and I greatly desired her anointing. She won my heart time after time, teaching after teaching. She had such vast information and knowledge, and I immersed myself in her intellect. I looked forward to the Sundays when she would get up to preach, because I knew I would be launched to another level of spirituality. "I will be your salvation until you find God for yourself!" she cried out while preaching one morning. I didn't really know what she meant, but she said it with fierceness behind her eyes and we all applauded in agreement. Critical questions about our leaders, doctrine, or policies were illegitimate. They were the pastors, and we dared not disagree with their truth.

Derek and I ministered to them during service. I was one of Dr. Sharon's assistants/intercessors, while Derek was Pastor George's personal armor bearer. This was an honor and a privilege that we did not take lightly. We loved our pastors and held them in the utmost esteem.

Indoctrination

We were taught that we must be cleansed of all filthiness of the flesh and spirit so that we might perfect holiness in the fear of God (2 Corinthians 7:1) and that if we wanted to see God move in our lives, we had to prove to God that we were ready for Him to use us by being holy. I prayed hard, travailed hard, and fasted until my bones literally ached. I was living what I thought was a consecrated lifestyle that God would be pleased with.

I had the notion that doing things would win God's attention and His approval of my life, so I constantly struggled to keep Him pleased. My own works of righteousness made the finished work of Jesus Christ null and void in a sense. The wholeness of His grace and redemption had never been the focal point. Grace and redemption had become a foreign language that I did not comprehend.

Scriptures like James 2:17, 1 Corinthians 9:27, and Philippians 2:12 were reinforced time and time again. I took these Scriptures at face value, totally misunderstanding their context, and they were articulated in a way that brought condemnation to my soul. Consider the verse from James:

"Even so faith, if it hath not works, is dead, being alone."

My false interpretation: Prove to God you have faith by your works.

The true context: Do not only confess faith, but act accordingly. If a person has a need, help him. If he is naked, don't just pray for him but clothe him.

And 1 Corinthians 9:27:
"But I keep under my body, and bring it into subjection: lest that by any means, when I have preached to others, I myself should be a castaway."

My false interpretation: I should punish myself because of my sinful nature.

The true context: Paul kept himself subjected and accountable to God. He was aware that it was important for him to practice what he preached so that he himself would not be disqualified from leading the church.

And Philippians 2:12:

"Wherefore, my beloved, as ye have always obeyed, not as in my presence only, but now much more in my absence, work out your own salvation with fear and trembling."

My false interpretation: I should work to seek God's love and approval.

The true context: Obedience comes through the process of sanctification, not salvation.

I devoured every word and every teaching as if my life depended on it. I put my total trust in the pastors because they were superior. They carried an air of authority so strong that it was almost frightening at times. As a new member, I noticed that the other members appeared to be timid and fearful, showing great obeisance to the pastors.

"Why does everybody seem so afraid?" I asked Dr. Sharon.

"They are not fearful," she said. "It's you and your negative perception."

"Oh."

I trusted her judgment, and I respected her position as my leader, never wanting to say or do anything against her. I was just a new member coming into something that was already established and I dared not ask challenging questions. They knew the word much better than I did, and I was determined to grasp every concept, every instruction, every teaching, and every interpretation like a baby who eats everything they're being fed. I didn't even take the time to chew it because it tasted so good to me. I just ate and ate and ate some more. I learned about leadership, servanthood, submission to authority, being a sacrifice, dying to self (in the sense of embracing God's will for my life rather than my own will), spiritual birthing (birthing one's gift through prayer), fasting, prayer, intercession, travailing, giving, tithing, worship, Levitical priesthood (worshipers' serving in the church), and so forth.

Thing were going great for us and we were growing spiritually as our hearts ignited with a passion to know Scripture and live according to every word we heard. We were blessed to have two cars, food on the table, and a decent home to live in. On Sundays we would eat out with the pastors and their seven daughters to get to know each other better. Their oldest daughter, Jayleen, was married and had two young children. She and her husband got along well with Derek and me, maybe because we were a married couple with a young child as well. One day Jayleen's husband expressed to Derek that he and his wife were facing financial trouble and that his mother and father-in-law had to drive them everywhere they needed to go because they didn't have a vehicle of their own. Derek's heart went out to him and he suggested that Jayleen and her husband use one of our cars for a few months so they'd have a means to get around the city. We could manage with one vehicle since we both worked on the military base at the time. So Derek typed up a three-month lease for them to sign.

As it turned out, three months turned into six months; with an addendum added to it, but we didn't mind. We were happy to be of help.

Chapter 3

Behavior Control

I learned the ways of the church, the ins and outs, the do's and don'ts, how to be and how not to be, what to wear and what not to wear, how to speak and how not to speak. We practically lived at the church, attending every prayer call, church meeting, small conference, and sabbatical (corporate church shut-ins that lasted twenty-one to forty days) and participating in every event. Every time the doors were opened, we were there, committed to serving and being expected to serve.

Dr. Sharon told me I needed to join the praise and worship team and participate in intercessory prayer and women's ministry. I also served on the children's ministry team and the altar worker team and worked in the office, the fine arts department, the bookstore, the prayer call center, the School of the Prophets, and the outreach program. We had dedicated our lives to the pastors for the sole purpose of honoring the Christ within them. If they said jump, we said, "How high?" If they said swim, we said, "How far?" They insisted that we honor the Christ in them by showing obeisance toward them.

They had become the most important people in our lives. They had priority over our marriage, our child, and all that we did. We didn't get out or spend family time and never thought to do so. Our schedule consisted of work, home, and church. We didn't do anything without asking them first, and we were OK with that.

However, my career started to conflict with the demands of our new church because the military has demands of its own. Dr. Sharon suggested that I separate from the military in order to be closer to her, but my goal was to become an Air Force chief one day, and I was adamant about my studies to make rank.

One morning I walked into my office to find all the staff there with big smiles on their faces.

"What's going on?" I asked.

"Congratulations," the lieutenant colonel said as he placed a certificate of promotion in my hand and said I had passed my exam for staff sergeant. All my studying had paid off. I was elated to hear the news and couldn't wait to put on rank.

I was pregnant with my second child at this time and had the opportunity to voluntarily separate from the Air Force in order to take care of my baby when she arrived. I felt torn between my career and my commitment to the church because Dr. Sharon kept advising me to be obedient to the Lord and separate from the military. I smiled and nodded each time she mentioned it, wondering if that was God's will for my life.

When I asked my husband what he thought about the idea of my separating from the military, he quickly answered no. The military was our primary source of income, he said, and we would need the support to take care of our baby in the coming months. Separating from the military just wouldn't be a wise decision for us.

But then I thought about faith. If it was God's will for me to separate, He would sustain us. I tried to convince Derek of this, but the bottom line was that he didn't think it would be good for us financially.

Dr. Sharon became more persistent in her approach. She would say things in front of the other women of the church like, "Everyone reaches out to me and wants to be close to me except for Dee" or "I don't know what I've ever done to Dee, but I guess she just doesn't want to be close."

But I did want to be close to her, so I approached my husband again, saying that I thought it was God's will for me to get out of the military and that we should trust God. "If Dr. Sharon is saying it, then it must be so." I said that I had a calling and that God was giving me a way to fulfill my purpose. I wanted him to understand that maybe the Lord was promoting me in ministry. Dr. Sharon was a woman of God who was highly admired and respected in the church, and she'd asked me to be close to her. It was a big deal to me. This was like being close to the prophet Elijah in my eyes.

Ultimately, I realized that Dr. Sharon had become more important to me than my promotion in the military, and I wanted to please her. Regardless of the fact that I was up for promotion in a couple of months, I went ahead and signed voluntary termination papers to end my military contract. Though he wasn't in full agreement with this, Derek didn't interfere with my decision because he knew it had been suggested by Dr. Sharon, who was all-seeing and all-knowing in our eyes, and he knew it meant a lot to me to be in the will of God.

But my decision affected Derek as well because he worked on the military base, and if I was no longer assigned to the base, he was no longer permitted to work on base. However, the Lord blessed Derek with a job working in Denver as a corrections officer a few weeks before my final separation. Denver is about an hour out from Colorado Springs, though, and I would no longer have a way to get to and from work every day. In light of this, we needed to revisit the contract concerning the lease of our other vehicle, so we told Jayleen and her husband about our situation and they agreed to return the vehicle.

Later that day, I received a call from Pastor George about the vehicle and the contract we had signed. He explained that a contract is legal and binding until it is fulfilled.

"You don't want to get the courts involved, do you?" he asked.

"No," I said.

"So I suggest you stick with the deal."

I got his drift. They would take us to court for asking for our vehicle back.

So I stuck it out, seven months pregnant and all. I asked friends and co-workers to take me to and from work until my final separation date, which was about a month away.

The College Loan

One evening while Derek was at work, I received a phone call from Pastor George. I was full of excitement! I couldn't believe he was calling me, of all people. What an honor.

He asked how I was doing and then proceeded to tell me he needed a favor.

"OK!" I said.

"How is your credit score?" he said.

"I think it's good," I said and told him my score.

He said he didn't think that would help him. "How is your husband's credit?"

"I know for sure Derek's is pretty good."

"Do you think your husband would mind if I used him to co-sign a loan?"

"Of course not," I told him, though I didn't know the stipulations of a co-sign.

He asked for Derek's social security number and I happily gave it to him. Then he handed the phone to one of his daughters and she proceeded to gather information from me. I asked her what this was all about and she told me that the loan was for her college, in the amount of $28,000. I'd been under the impression that the loan was for Pastor George because he was the one who'd called. I proceeded to give his daughter our information; after all, he was the pastor and I trusted him.

Immediately after we got off the phone, I called my husband at work and told him how I'd been able to help Pastor George. When I told him about the co-sign, there was a long silence.

"Dee! What have you done?" Derek finally said.
"I thought you'd be happy!" I said.
"No, I'm not. Do you even know what a co-sign is?"
"No, not really. I didn't think it was really a big deal."
"Well, you don't have to do it."
"You already told him yes, and I don't want Pastor George to be angry with me if I don't go through with it. I don't want that kind of trouble."

> "Banks require a co-sign when they don't trust the person's payment history, which is a sure sign that you should not trust it either. I learned the hard lesson of putting trust in man."
>
> -Dave Ramsey

"Do not put your trust in princes, in human beings, who cannot save." (Psalm 146:3)

This decision has crippled our financial status and the loan continues to grow due to non-payment.

Financial Struggle

My husband had been working in Denver for about a year by now, and we weren't able to make ends meet because I wasn't working. Our finances fell significantly behind, but I wasn't worried because I felt that I had given up something I truly loved in order to serve God. Finally, several months later, Derek got the opportunity to take a contracting job in Iraq. This was it—our big break! We'd be able to pay the debts we'd incurred. Derek was willing to make the sacrifice of leaving his family for a year to rebuild our finances. It was a bittersweet moment for us, but we knew God would sustain us. We called the pastors to let them know Derek would be going to Iraq, and they celebrated with us.

A couple of weeks later, Pastor George called Derek and asked him to meet him at the church. When they met, Derek was instructed to make a separate allotment to the pastor's bank account while he was in Iraq in order for him to receive a portion of Derek's income. "My wife told me to tell you that sons take care of their father, so it is your duty to take care of me," he said. "I need you to think of how much you're going to sow monthly to me and let me know how much it will be."

When Derek shared this with me, my heart sank within my soul. I had just recently given birth to our beautiful baby, Naomi, and we'd been racking up credit-card charges in order to provide for her. How were we going to take care of the pastor on top of all our other debts? I sat in my rocking chair and cried. I knew their standards, and whatever we decided to give had better be significant. For fear of saying no, we said yes. We felt the pressure to give big or be chastised for not meeting their standards.

In the end, we gave fifty percent of my husband's monthly income. And we continued to give our tithes and offerings and sowed various seeds to bless them whenever we could. It was our responsibility as sons and daughters to give to the kingdom and take care of the man and woman of God. They were a family of eleven members, including two grandbabies. We gave two thousand dollars a month to Pastor George and several hundred to the church, and by this time our house went into foreclosure and our vehicle was repossessed. We ultimately ended up filing for bankruptcy after seeking counsel from Pastor George first. He recommended that we use his bankruptcy lawyer to file suit.

Pastor George taught that we should have faith enough to give even if it was our electricity bill since we didn't have enough to pay it anyway. For instance, his concept was, if the utility bill was due and you only had half of the money for it; negate paying the utility bill and sow the half payment into the kingdom and God will honor your faith. We adhered to his ideologies and struggled to maintain our finances.

After several months, I called Derek in Iraq, crying about our finances and how I had no money to put toward our household bills. We agreed that we were no longer able to give the amount we had agreed to give Pastor George. Derek advised that I give the pastors a call and explain our situation and said he, too, would call Pastor George the next evening.

The next day I mustered up the courage to call Pastor George and let him know that we could no longer afford to give fifty percent of our income but that we would continue to give a lesser portion. I was so nervous that I was shaking.

When Pastor George answered the phone, I began to explain things to him and he placed me on speakerphone. Dr. Sharon was outraged! She angrily shouted at me in the background.

"If you were really prophetic, you would know that you are sowing into your future! Your faith is small!"

They drilled and scolded me for about an hour, telling me how disappointed they were in me. Sobbing, I felt horrible, but at that time my other vehicle was in repossession status because we were giving so much to the pastors. The only thing I could do was pull back some. My husband was a contractor making more than enough in Iraq, and we were at home struggling to buy toilet paper and groceries. There had been many times when I had to ask Pastor George for money to buy food to sustain my daughters and me. I'd had to borrow gas money to get to and from church services. It just didn't make any sense to me—how was it that we sowed and sowed but we weren't reaping a harvest?

Later, on an occasion when I was alone with Pastor George, I timidly raised the question. He was a little easier to approach than Dr. Sharon.

"Why am I not reaping a harvest?" I asked

He looked at me and drew his eyebrows down in irritation. "I told you this before. You are sowing toward your future. I'm not going to go over this with you again."

Church Pillars

Those of us whose husbands were in Iraq were called Pillars of the church because of our financial contribution, and we were proud of that. But we competed against one another, striving to be that true son or daughter to the pastors. There was jealousy among us, and whoever the pastors pulled in close was envied. It was all about who could sow the largest seed. If someone sowed a large seed, it was announced to the congregation as if that person were the only one truly taking care of our leaders. This not only heightened the level of envy and jealousy but also propagated feelings of guilt, inadequacy, and failure.

Chapter 4

Emotional Control

Dr. Sharon asked that I write a profile of my life revealing all that I had been through, all the hurts and pains, in order for her to get to know me better and minister to me accordingly. I spent a week or two writing down all that I could remember about growing up and the things I had faced. I thought it was a great idea. I handed my profile to her with excitement, looking forward to her opinion on the things I had disclosed. She took it and promised to get back to me.

Months went by and she never said a word about it. I figured she was busy running the church, so I didn't mention it. But I noticed dramatic changes in not only how she treated me but also in how her seven daughters treated me. They ranged in age from seven to twenty-three, and they all seemed to have sat around the table and read about me. One daughter made snickering comments on things that I had written for Dr. Sharon and mocked me as she and her sisters giggled. I was humiliated.

It was as if I'd given away something precious and it had been used for my ruin. I realized that I had allowed them into the deep places of my heart. I was being defined by my past and felt as if they had some kind of hold over me. My very words were being used against me, which took a great toll on me, and I became extremely anxious and nervous.

The girls were vicious, to say the least. The oldest daughters sought opportunities to destroy my character, creating lies and twisting my words. They kept tabs on me for their parents, reporting who I spoke to, what I wore, and where I went. For instance, if one of the church members invited me to her house for dinner, Dr. Sharon knew about it.

I was called into Dr. Sharon's office on many occasions with scoldings that ripped holes in my heart. Sometimes I would get caught in the middle of baffling he said/she said arguments brought on by the daughters. These girls were very crafty and knew how to turn absolutely nothing into something. Every time they came near me, I trembled with anxiety. I never knew what they would conjure up next.

I went from being somewhat confident to being overly submissive and timid. I didn't want to upset the girls or their mother. I became what they wanted me to be. I was ridiculed, lied about, used, abused, made fun of, accused, condemned, misunderstood, tricked, taken advantage of, abandoned, financially raped, hated, envied, scolded, rebuked, punished, and mentally, emotionally, and verbally abused—all within the four walls of the church.

I lost my confidence and self-esteem within the first two years of joining this organization. I had been scolded so much that my spirit felt as if it were shattered. I no longer recognized myself internally or externally. My pastors had become my mom and dad, and they referred to themselves as such. Pastor George always reminded us that he was our spiritual father and that we must show him honor and obeisance. We literally bowed down to them on our hands and knees, honoring them as if they were our King and Queen. It felt strange at first, but eventually I became accustomed to it.

My birth parents had become outsiders. I was instructed not to communicate with them, because they did not understand the religious group I was in. They became intruders, and if I let them into my life they would sabotage my destiny. They were the enemy. So I kept them at bay. I had become fearful, just like I'd noticed the other members were when we first started attending services. My every move was monitored. I was told that in order to remain consecrated and separated before God, I could not socialize and have friends. I didn't want to incur any hostility from them, so I submitted to their authority at all times.

The church conducted two Sunday services and I attended both, not to mention the leadership service that preceded them at seven-thirty. One Sunday I decided to stay for the leadership service and the first service only. I was exhausted after being badgered and ridiculed for not measuring up to the standards of God, so I went home and laid down.

Before I knew it, Pastor George was ringing my doorbell and banging at my door yelling for me to open up. I couldn't believe he was at my house. I was afraid because he was banging so hard. I sat there shushing my girls to keep them quiet until he left. I didn't open the door.

Later that evening, Dr. Sharon called me to tell me they were on their way to my house again because I had not been at the second service. When they arrived, they said that they could feel the devil and that he was thick in my house. That scared me. They asked why I hadn't attended second service and I told them that I'd felt ridiculed and badgered and that I was tired and wanted to go home. They said they needed to pray over me and my house because I had fought against them and now the devil was in my home and they needed to cast him out. They anointed my head with oil, prayed over me, my daughters, and my home, and before I knew it I was crying and apologizing for leaving service early.

I no longer trusted myself, my thoughts, my ideas, or my decisions. I went to the pastors for everything and soon lost the ability to make my own choices. I noticed that my voice would even change when they came around. It became high-pitched and squeaky whenever I spoke to them, which was odd because my voice is naturally low-pitched and mellow.

I bowed down and humbled myself before them, giving them total control and rule over me for fear of getting into some type of trouble. I had no voice; my confidence was shattered to pieces, and I stayed within the guidelines of what they wanted my character to be. Any time I appeared to be confident, it was noticed and quickly deemed to be unrighteous.

Although I was twenty-five years old, I felt like a child. I was fearful, nervous, and jumpy. My stomach flipped any time a member of the pastoral family spoke to me, because I didn't know what was coming. I didn't want my words to be twisted. I felt like a little girl looking for approval from Mommy and Daddy. They completely had my heart, and I trusted them. They became my world, and I had become a byproduct of abusive leadership constructed through manipulation and control. I had succumbed to it in the name of being a good Christian.

I submitted to abusive authority because I did not try every spirit to see if they were of God. I'd put my trust in man, making him lord of my life, and the enemy had deceived me. The Bible warns us of false prophets and teachers who deliver destructive heresies or doctrines to the believers.

> But there were also false prophets among the people, just as there will be false teachers among you. They will secretly introduce destructive heresies, even denying the sovereign Lord who bought them—bringing swift destruction on themselves.
> Many will follow their depraved conduct and will bring the way of truth into disrepute." (2 Peter 2:1-2)

False prophets and teachers misrepresent the truth, which is the word, which is Jesus Christ. They present themselves as God's representatives of truth, but in actuality they create religious lies that burden and condemn the people of God. The people submit themselves under the spirit of control and manipulation, thus becoming yoked to destructive oppression in the name of following and being good servants of the Lord.

Jesus tells us that His yoke is easy and his burden is light. (Matthew 11:30)

It's so important to know the word of God for yourself. Many have become blinded by deception and the misconstrued word. False teachers become lord over the people instead of leading the people to the lordship of Jesus Christ through love. The Bible tells us that many will follow their destructive ways, and unfortunately, I was one who followed. I was denying the lordship of Jesus Christ over my life even though I thought I was serving the Lord to the highest degree. I gave man supreme authority over my life, which rejects the redemption of Jesus. I was quickly perishing for lack of knowledge.

The pain of religious cruelty was the deepest pain I had ever known. I was devastated by the endless accusations against me. It just wouldn't stop. No matter what I said or did, my words and intentions were used against me. I tried hard to be loved and accepted by the church leaders because I had so much respect for their knowledge of Scripture and the weight of authority they carried. The Lord used them mightily in prayer and deliverance, and I was awestruck.

But the more I glorified them, the worse things became. I was confused because I didn't understand how people could be anointed and at the same time so cruel and hateful. I wasn't supposed to be going through these things, not in the church. I'd thought that church people who love the Lord were compassionate, loving, and gentle toward one another. Boy, was I rudely awakened.

The pastors built people up, tore them back down, and then built them up and tore them down again. It was a vicious circle. As a result, we would gain confidence from them only and seek their approval. There were many, many instances where I was accused and ridiculed for things I hadn't done. It seemed that my words were twisted and used against me every time I spoke, so I learned to be very careful when speaking. I didn't understand what was going on. I often felt confused and muddled.

When I'd been stationed in Japan, I felt so free. I would walk with the Lord and talk with Him. I was in daily communion with Him. He spoke to my heart and showed me things beyond my comprehension. Now, I still enjoyed my prayer times with Him, but it had become a repetitious duty without fulfillment.

Stricken With Strife

One day after church service, Jayleen asked me to go to lunch with her. We had been to lunch in the past, and each time I was extremely uncomfortable because she wasn't especially fond of her mother and sisters and would express that to me. But I was never clear on her intentions; she, too, would have me hemmed up in a mess of unwanted trouble with twisted lies.

She was only a few years younger than me and by now we both had two young children, so we could relate to one another. I tried to be a friend and listened as she vented her frustrations, not saying a word for fear that my encouragement would be twisted one way or another.

Later that same day, the youth pastor also asked me to come over so we could practice a praise dance for an upcoming church event. I let Jayleen know that I would be practicing with the youth pastor and that we would have to reschedule lunch for later in the week, and she seemed to be OK with it.

I was a little nervous about going to the youth pastor's house because getting together with another person from the church was more or less prohibited. Dr. Sharon had made it clear that I could not have any friends in my life, and I didn't want to be accused of not being consecrated. I hadn't fellowshipped in a long time, but I'd figured this would be OK because it was dance practice and we had met for practice at the church before for youth events.

When I arrived at her house, we began to discuss several ideas and dance choices. She was a dancer herself and loved to give tips and advice on certain songs and movements. She'd always been nice and down to earth, laughing and making jokes at any given time. Her personality was light and refreshing, and she related to the youths extremely well. She took her leadership role seriously and was there for them through thick and thin. I could tell that she truly cared about the kids, and I respected her for being such a positive voice influence in their lives.

At one point, she asked me if I had heard about any trouble concerning her. I could tell she was a little nervous as she began to share that Dr. Sharon had reprimanded her a couple of days earlier. During youth service, one of the pastors' daughters accused her of inappropriate teaching and reported it to her mother. She said that accusations were being made against her and that her words were being twisted. She said the pastors' daughter had gotten into some kind of mischief and began to tell lies about her to save herself from trouble. She was distraught as she poured out her heart to me.

I was frozen after hearing her words. *Why me?* I felt stuck, like I wanted to run but I couldn't. So I stood there and I listened to her troubles. I didn't want to be afraid of what she had to say, but I was.

Because I had experienced their chastisement on several counts, my heart went out to her and I could see that she was extremely bothered by this. I let her know how I identified with this. I told her how the daughter had intimidated me beyond words. I was fearful and defenseless half the time, jumping at the daughters' every command for fear of being punished or shunned by their parents.

I encouraged her to talk to the pastors after everything settled down, and she said she would consider it. Before I left, she pleaded with me not to let the pastors know she'd told me. I gave her my word.

That night when I got home, my phone rang. At first I thought it was the youth pastor calling to thank me for listening, so I hurriedly answered it, but to my surprise it was Dr. Sharon. My heart stopped.

"I know where you went and who you spoke to," she said firmly.

I couldn't breathe.

"I had a vision that a dark angel struck your heart with a fiery dart and turned you against me. I need to meet with you as soon as possible."

My stomach turned. I stood there petrified.

So we scheduled a meeting for the next day during Bible study service.

Judas

"What did the youth pastor tell you?" Dr. Sharon immediately asked when we met. She stared at me with discontent; her dark piercing eyes penetrated the core of my soul. I began to tremble uncontrollably. I tried to speak, but I stumbled over my words. My eyes filled with tears. I couldn't tell her.

I let her know that she and her daughters intimidated me and how fearful I was.

She appeared to be amused by this, as her lips curled up into a slight smile.

"I'll talk to them," she slowly replied. "You are mistaking fear for reverence. What you are describing as fear is a holy fear, in reverence to me because I carry God's anointing."

After this, I was confused as I tried to gather my thoughts. I was petrified by her, but I took her word for it. I knew I had to honor her and all that she stood for. So I apologized for talking with the youth pastor.

"That's OK, dear." She said this situation was proof that I could not have friends in my life, because people were out to destroy me. Then she grabbed my hands. "Well, let's pray." She prayed against the evil onslaught of the devil and then warned me not to communicate with that sister again, reiterating that I could not have friends and must remain consecrated.

By now Bible study was ending. As we walked out of the office, heads turned, and Dr. Sharon approached the pulpit. She stood waiting patiently for her husband to finish the prayer and then announced to the church with tears in her eyes, "We have a Judas in our midst ..."

She glared at me, making it clear to the congregation who Judas was.

"Ungodly conversation took place to where our pastoral family has been attacked," she said.

I gasped. *What just happened? Who's Judas? This has got to be some kind of joke! I'm not Judas. Judas betrayed Jesus with a kiss. Judas purchased a field with the wages of iniquity.*

I was confused. A painful bubble of air rose in my throat. I could hardly breathe.

This is a mistake. I don't want to be Judas, of all things. Not Judas!

Shunned

Sure enough, talk spread through the church and I was thereafter shunned for having been corrupted. Weeks went by and nobody spoke to me. Everyone walked right by me as if I weren't there. Until one day when Pastor George approached me. "You know I love you, right?" he said.

I looked up at him, starving for his acceptance and desperate for the shunning to finally be over. He suggested that I fast until corruption was cut out of me, and I felt as if I had fallen into some kind of deep pit.

As the shunning continued, I was reminded how detestable I was by stares, comments, and judgments. It went on for so long that I began to hate myself. The more I pleaded my innocence, the worse it became. To others I was deceptive, abominable, vicious, full of the devil, insecure, passive, and on and on. I pleaded and cried for forgiveness, but nothing I said mattered.

My heart ached for months. I needed them to love me, accept me, validate me, know me, and comfort me. I apologized over and over to try to resolve the issue, but my apologies were not accepted, and the congregation stayed away from me as if I had the plague. I tried to explain that I'd never spoken against leadership, but the mere fact that I sat and listened to the youth pastor was perceived as a betrayal, which signaled my corruption.

I fasted for days on end, limiting myself to water. I lost so much weight that my clothes hung off my waist. Nobody noticed, nobody cared, and nobody knew my pain. One day after church, I went home and shut myself in my dark basement and cried out to God to deliver me. I felt like scum in His eyes.

I attended 5 a.m. prayer every Tuesday and Thursday, determined to prove to the church and to God that He could trust me again as His servant. Approaching the altar to pray was the hardest thing in the world because the intercessors thought I had the devil inside me. They glared at me, despising me, while praying prayers over the microphone to cast the devil out. One woman approached me, wrapped her hands around my face, and, shaking my head to and fro, commanded a wicked spirit to come out. I sobbed in disbelief. I was broken in spirit, and my heart ached with despair.

"Why is this happening to me?" I cried.

I threw myself onto the altar praying and asked God for understanding. Why had He placed me in a den of wolves?

[Side Note]Even if you've never experienced the kind of humiliation I did at that altar, you may be publicly or privately accused of doing evil. Be strong and let the Lord lead you through those difficult times. When false accusations are made against you, trust God to vindicate you.

Chapter 5

Fellowship in His Suffering

During this time, I got to know the Lord in ways I'd never imagined. He became my refuge, my strength, my strong tower, and my way of escape. I was no longer joyfully singing in his presence but travailing, wailing, and fighting for my sanity in His presence. I was in a dark place, a place where I could fellowship only in his suffering—the suffering referred to in Philippians 3:10:

"I want to know Christ—yes, to know the power of his resurrection and participation in his sufferings, becoming like him in his death."

I had become a partner in unfavorable sorrow with Him, but I found pockets of peace and rest in Him in the midst of the turbulence that surrounded my life. I had never experienced brokenness like this before. I wasn't just financially broken but also spiritually. I felt bankrupt even with all the praying, all the fasting, all the giving, and all the serving, I was not at peace, and it was through this season of suffering that God anointed me for ministry.

I felt like an olive that had been crushed, and the crushing had caused me to seek God diligently and fervently because I had nothing else to lean on. When I sought Him, He poured out His spirit on me, allowing me to enter into heavenly places with Him. This was the start of an intimate relationship with the Lord.

In my season of brokenness, He gave me a prophetic dance that flowed through my bones, causing the atmosphere to shift under the anointing and allowing deliverance to take place in my heart and within the congregation. It was like fire shut up in my bones.

Dancing was my way of expressing my love for Him and the relationship we had begun to develop. He gave me the "Divine Mime." Yes, mime, the art of interpretive dance with the use of white paint to enhance facial expression. It was in prayer that I had a vision of miming under the power of God. I didn't know how to mime, and it wasn't something I'd ever dreamed of doing, but it soon became a part of my ministry. This gift truly made room for me. The Lord used what appeared to be a foolish thing to confound the wise.

Me. I was the foolish thing. I was the passive jelly-backed girl who ran from confrontation at any given cost, the quiet one who dared not speak for fear of sounding different. The Lord saw fit to rest his anointing on me in the area of dance to break oppressive chains and set captives free in the spirit.

Acceptance

The day of the church's anniversary dinner, I wanted to die, but I made myself go. I would do anything to be accepted again. During the reception, before the guest speaker spoke, the hostess asked if anyone had words of appreciation for the pastors. My heart started thundering in my chest, and I felt the Holy Spirit nudging me toward the opportunity to make things right. I didn't want to go forward, but I couldn't stop the intense pounding in my chest, nudging me to move.

Before I knew it, I was walking to the front of the room. I could hear laughing and mocking as I approached the front, but I didn't care. I was determined to get things right. The hostess handed me the microphone and I began to speak,

"I know this is the church anniversary dinner, but ..." The tears began to form and I began to repent in front of everybody, not pleading my case, just sobbing in repentance. I asked for forgiveness from the bottom of my heart. I took full responsibility even though I believed I was innocent. I honored the pastors so much that I couldn't imagine deliberately hurting them. I loved them so deeply it hurt. They had my heart in their hands, period.

For the first time in months, Dr. Sharon smiled at me. "I'm proud of you."

When she spoke, I felt the life come back into my body. Her words literally meant everything in the world to me. I felt as if this woman possessed a part of me. The fact that she spoke to me released the pain from my heart.

The guest speaker then called out to me. "Apostle! You did a great act of repentance."

I looked at him in disbelief, wondering why he'd called me "apostle."

"You just opened up the floor for my message, which I no longer have to preach," he said. "I want you to stand up here and pray for others who need to be released from guilt and shame."

One by one, people began to come up for prayer, including the youth pastor. The guest pastor had me touch and pray for each person at the altar. In that moment, I realized the Lord was using my suffering to set others free. I was astonished.

[Side note] "Whenever you put man on a pedestal, you reject God's grace, love, and acceptance over you."

Mom's Visit

Thanksgiving was right around the corner, and my mom decided to take a flight to Colorado to see me and meet her grandbabies for the first time. It had been six or seven years since we had seen each other, and I tried to stop her. I didn't want her to come because I knew how she felt about my church, and in my eyes she was coming to sow a seed of deception. I didn't want any more drama in my life, especially after what I had just come out of.

I told her it wasn't a good time for the girls and me and that I would most likely be spending Thanksgiving with my pastors since Derek was still in Iraq. However, my mother told me she was coming anyway because she believed the Lord had told her to come and there was something I was to receive from her coming.

Anxiety hit me like a ton of bricks. I was petrified. *She can't come here!* I tried my best to stop her. I told her she needed rest. I told her I wasn't cooking this year or doing anything big, but she persisted.

When she stepped off the plane, she looked amazing. She was radiant, stunning, joyous, and free. I told her how beautiful and alive she looked, and she regarded me with concern.

"Well ... you look kind of homely." She was obviously taken aback by my appearance. My clothes were worn and old, and I was thin and a little frazzled. But at the time, I didn't know what she was talking about. I hadn't noticed the changes.

She went to church with me an hour early that Sunday for our intercessory prayer, during which another elder and I rotated in prayer for an hour before leadership class. My mother watched as I took the microphone and began to pray. She sat quietly praying and weeping at the same time. She said she was pleased with the woman of God I had become.

During the actual church service, my mother sat with no expression on her face most of the time while Pastor George delivered his message. Occasionally, she'd frown and then raise her eyebrows in an expression of shock. For the first time, I saw Pastor George struggle through a sermon. He didn't have the effect on the people that he usually did. I wondered if my mother's being there was distracting him. He glared at me throughout his sermon, and I squirmed nervously.

When the service was over, my mother walked up to Pastor George and introduced herself while I tended to the CD/DVD table. She pulled a book out of her purse called *Purifying the Altar*, by Al Houghton, and handed it to him. He took the book, smiled, and walked into his office. I could have fainted! My heart raced as I ran over to her.

"Mom, what did you do?" I cried.

"I just gave him a book to read. There's no crime in that," she said with a smile.

I couldn't believe it. I was so upset with her that I wanted to cry. She didn't understand the way things worked here. I felt sick with the thought of being in trouble with the leaders again.

After a few days, she told me she had something to share with me. I told her that if it was about my church, I didn't want to hear it. But she proceeded to show me anyway.

"Look," she said.

So I glanced at the website she had pulled up on the computer.

I gasped. The writing in big red letters said "Religious Cult Tactics," and there was a list of methods such as mind alteration, coercion, brainwashing, mind control, and thought reform. The website described the character of a cult leader as that of "a strong authority figure that uses deception and manipulation to expand their influence for the purpose of power and money."

The page looked something like this:

Religious Cult Tactics

Behavior Control
- Where, how, and with whom members live and associate.
- What clothing, colors, and hairstyles to wear.
- Which foods/drinks are accepted or rejected.
- How much financial dependence recruits are to have on the group, what percentage of recruits' income is collected for the group's purposes.
- How much time is spent on leisure activities such as relaxing, sleeping, and vacationing.

Information Control
- Deception—lie to obtain their goal.
- Outside Information Forbidden—written critiques, letters, editorials, or history of involvements of former members of the group.
- Levels of Information—leaders are seen as possessing "sacred science," or having the ability to decipher and interpret doctrines, philosophies, and so forth, in a way that no one else has ever done or could ever do.
- Spying and Surveillance—system of monitoring, reporting deviant thoughts, feelings, and actions to leadership.
- Group Propaganda—misquotations, statements taken out of context from non-cult sources.
- Non-confidential Confessions—information about "sins" is used to abolish identity boundaries.
- Past "sins" are used to manipulate and control; no forgiveness or absolution is given.

Thought Control
- No critical questions about the leader, doctrine, or policy are seen as legitimate.
- No alternative belief systems are viewed as legitimate, good, or useful.

Emotional Control
- Guilt Association
  - Who you are (and why you are not living up to your potential).
  - Who your family is (those from dysfunctional families are to attribute their dysfunctional pasts to their not being a member of the group yet).
  - What secrets lie in your past (sexual history, childhood mistakes, any past criminal involvement is overly emphasized).

- With whom you are affiliated (the company you keep, boyfriend/girlfriend/fiancées shunned, family, friends, etc.).
- What you think (how you feel and what you do about your feelings, whether what you think and feel is acceptable to the group).
- Fear Induction
  - Fear of thinking independently. (Recruits wonder whether they are making right decisions, what the consequences will be if they think independently.)
  - Fear of losing salvation. (Recruits are taught that salvation is attained only through group affiliation and nowhere else.)
  - Fear of being shunned. (Recruits often risk losing family, friends, job, etc. if they decide to leave. Many cults "mark" or otherwise collectively shun former members.)
  - Fear of disapproval. (Recruits learn to live according to the laws of the leaders, and learn that deviating from these laws is detrimental to the well-being of both oneself and the others in the group.)
- Extremism
  - Extremes of emotional highs and lows (rewards and punishments go hand in hand).
  - Ritual and often public confessions of sins (confessions provoked and exaggerated by inductor).
  - "We/they" mentality, in which group sees itself as better than the rest of the world. The group sees itself as the only people capable of accurate doctrinal interpretation (also called "sacred science").
- Phobia Indoctrination
  - Phobia indoctrination is the programming of irrational fears of ever leaving the group, or even questioning the leadership's authority. Recruits are manipulated to the extent that they cannot visualize

> a positive and successful future without being in the group. They are taught that horrific consequences will ensue if they are to leave (i.e., "hell," "demon possession," accidents, suicide, and/or insanity, etc.).

My heart sank. "I can't read this," I said. It was too much to take in, so I turned off the computer. I stared at the wall, feeling angry and confused. I completely identified with every description on the list, but I didn't want to believe I was involved in a cult. So I blocked the thought from my mind.

My pastors are right. My mother is full of deceptive lies, and she's just jealous of my relationship with them. I dismissed the insidious idea of being involved in a cult, because I was smarter than that. I was ready for my mother to go home because I thought she had brought confusion into my life—God certainly wasn't the author of confusion. I believed the devil was using her, and I wanted no part of it.

So I continued to walk in the way I knew to be true. By now I had gained further approval from my leaders. I believed that I was growing spiritually and that the ministry was going to bring me into my true purpose and destiny. I was in a lifelong covenant with the church leaders and couldn't fathom ever leaving. I was being used in the prophetic mime dance and was often called on to do Bible study reviews. They trusted me and I trusted them. As long as I stayed away from other people, all was well. I didn't have any problem with separating myself from family or friends as long as I had the pastors' approval.

Chapter 6

The Enslaved Mind-Set

When I hear the word *slavery* I think of bondage, captivity, oppression, servitude, suppression, repression, and so forth. My mind naturally reverts back to African slaves who were brought to America against their will. I think of Harriet Tubman, who like Moses was called to set the captives free. However, she was born into slavery herself. She escaped from her plantation in Maryland by following the North Star, which enabled her to discover a route to freedom that led her to Philadelphia.

Harriet Tubman didn't just go on with her life from there, though. She returned to the trenches, endangering her life in order to lead other slaves to freedom. She received visions and dreams from God, which I believe gave her the courage to take a stand against slavery. She delivered hundreds of slaves to freedom, making nineteen trips to the South. Although there were risky routes to find safe houses and safe transportation, she was determined to live freely and to lead others to their freedom.

I can't imagine the fear they faced in their pursuit of freedom. I'm sure some wanted to go back because the route to freedom was too hard and slavery was all they knew. I'm sure they were overwhelmed by the fear of getting caught and the thought of what would happen to them after being caught. Not to mention the challenges they still had to face when they became free, like finding a home, earning wages, and adjusting to their freedom.

The spiritual journey of becoming free from the religious mind-set is like a journey on the Underground Railroad. Not everybody will approve of your coming out of religious formalities and traditions and coming into freedom and relationship in Christ. This is not a popular message; it's risky to even speak about these things, because it may inspire the religious slave owners to persecution for helping to lead their prisoners to freedom, but I'm a risk-taker.

The religious spirit comes to imprison the mind and enchain your thinking. One of Satan's favorite strategies is to imprison God's people in the very thing that we love and trust, our belief system. The very thing you love so much can be the same thing the enemy will use to keep you in bondage. You may be a disciplined Christian, and there's nothing wrong with that, but the enemy could use the fact that you're disciplined to impose excessive restrictions or limitations that confine you and imprison your thinking, which brings an imbalance to you.

You can become a slave to whatever you surrender yourself to without proper balance. The balance is *relationship* with Jesus Christ. Demonic powers come to steal, kill, and destroy, and what better way to deceive the church than to impart legalism (strict adherence to a literal interpretation of a law, rule, or religious or moral code), condemnation, and oppression through the preached word of God. Christians who have a passion for living a holy lifestyle for Christ can still be misled into thinking that it takes works and man's approval for God to move on their behalf if they don't have a proper understanding of what Christ did for them on the cross. As Acts 10:34 says, "God is no respecter of persons." He loves us and bestows his grace on us regardless of how perfect or imperfect we may be.

And as John 4:1-3 says, "Believe not every spirit, but try the spirits whether they are of God: because many false prophets have gone out into the world." As disheartening as this may sound, it is the truth; the Bible, if placed in the wrong hands, can be used as a vehicle to enforce false teaching and bring you under the snare of manipulation and control. Teachers, ministers, pastors, and other leaders with the wrong motives are capable of putting religious fetters on you to get you to do what they want you to do.

Some leaders use the Bible to accuse the brethren instead of leading them to the love of Christ and the sacrifice He made to save them. We are living in perilous times. Testing the spirits in Christian churches is an area that few people want to speak about. However, it must be addressed because Satan is operating through false teachers and seducing spirits. They are very real and very present in Christian churches today.

Manipulation was the snare that the enemy used to entrap me. Manipulation is to control as a control bar is to a puppet. The control bar is the instrument used to control the movement of a puppet. Think of manipulation as a thought or a word spoken. Words and thoughts have the ability to either release you to something or restrain you from something.

What thoughts control you? Who spoke those words over you? What motivates you? Are you driven by acceptance, approval, validation? Why do you strive for the things you strive for? What drives you to do the things you do?

I encourage you to write down these questions and answer them truthfully. No one needs to see what you write, so be true to yourself. For some it may be success, approval, or validation, and for others it may be fame, pride, or ego. Cast your cares upon the Lord who sustains and ask Him to guide you through all your endeavors.

* "Control and manipulation should not be what drives us; instead, we must allow the love of God to operate in our lives, which motivates us to carry out His will."

Self-indulgent Shepherds

Ezekiel 34 lets us know that it is possible for sheep (believers) to be enslaved by their shepherds (leaders). The Lord instructed

Ezekiel to prophesy against the shepherds, referring to the priests, the kings, and the prophets who fleeced the flocks for personal gain rather than leading them righteously.

Verse 2 says these shepherds of Israel fed themselves. They contrived their own ease, advantage, and honor. The Lord rebuked them who were more interested in taking care of themselves than in the well-being of their flock.

Verse 3 says they ate the fat and clothed themselves with the wool. This tells us the Lord is not pleased with shepherds who do well for themselves but neglect the needs of the sheep.

Verse 3 goes on to say, "Ye kill them that are fed." The rich and wealthy fell prey to these shepherds who contrived methods to take their lives and then their estates. These self-indulgent leaders neglected to lead, protect, watch over, and provide for their flock. They did not strengthen the weak or heal the sick. They did not go after the strays and the lost sheep. They ruled harshly and brutally and the sheep were therefore scattered.

Finally, verse 27b tells us what will happen to these sheep:

> "They will know that I am the Lord, when I break the bars of their yoke and rescue them from the hands of those who enslaved them."

You Have Placed Them Before Me

"You have placed them before me," the Lord said to me one day.

What do I do about this? I doubted that I'd actually heard the words from God.

I went to Dr. Sharon. "The Lord told me I've put you and Pastor George before Him," I said.

"You haven't placed us before God," she said. "The devil is trying to trick you in order to get you to break covenant with us."

I believed her and rebuked the devil.

"Do not worship any other god, for the Lord, whose name is Jealous, is a jealous God." (Exodus 34:14)

But the Lord continued to speak to my heart. *"You have placed them before me. There is more to it than just the four walls of the church, Dee."*

Whatever I choose to do or whatever career path I choose to take will involve ministry. Ministry is showing the love of Christ to others, whether it be consoling someone at work or buying flowers to cheer up your boss. Loving people brings joy to God's heart, and helping others pleases Him.

"What do you like to do, Dee?" He asked.

"I like to dance. I feel free when I dance," I said.

"Then dance. You've got to have balance."

The word *balance* rang in my spirit like Sunday-morning church bells, but I didn't know what to do with it. *I have no life outside of church. I don't even know the city of Colorado Springs. I haven't ventured out to see what the city has to offer. I've refrained from social activities in the name of consecration.*

Suddenly I felt confined, like I couldn't take a deep breath without somebody saying, "Don't you breathe that way!" Everything around me was church, prayer, travail, Bible study, fasting.

"Ballet!" I shouted, "I'll take ballet classes!"

So I took classes at a local ballet center every week. I felt freedom and the liberty to just be me for a change. I hadn't had this feeling in a long time, and I loved it. The class was full of people who loved to dance just like me, but I didn't know how to relate to them, because I couldn't have a normal conversation without speaking about my church or the Bible and God, so I just kept quiet and smiled. I enjoyed every minute of it.

At the same time, though, I felt guilty for having such a good time aside from my church. *What has my life become?* My very existence felt like a chore. I was not happy, nor did I know how to be happy anymore. *How is it that I'm doing everything in the name of God but there's no peace within me?*

Chapter 7

Coming Out!

I woke up one morning feeling as if something were extremely wrong. A cloud seemed to be hovering over me and I couldn't come out from under it. I continued to go to church but still couldn't shake this feeling that plagued me. This went on for about three weeks, and I couldn't connect or relate to the worship services no matter how hard I tried. I felt disconnected.

The people in the congregation would be jumping, crying, and shouting after the preached word went forth, but I felt nothing at all. I was numb. I sat and stared like a deer in headlights during every service. It was strange, to say the least. I searched for God, but I couldn't find Him in the sanctuary. I wanted to feel what everyone else was feeling, but I couldn't. I could see and hear Dr. Sharon preaching the word with great ambition to move the people with conviction, but I couldn't connect. I sat there like a bump on a log.

I kept asking myself what was wrong with me. *Have I all of a sudden become dull of hearing like the Bible says?* I was the only one sitting there with no emotion. I wasn't moved; I couldn't feel the Lord's presence at all. I didn't want the pastors to notice my awkward state, so I forced myself to cry as if I were in His presence. What's happening to me? I felt like I was on the outside of a window looking in at a movement that I wasn't a part of. For lack of a better term, I felt sober.

Risky Routes to Freedom

Meanwhile, I began to notice that my friend Marsha had not been to services for quite some time. This was strange because she'd attended faithfully and had been committed to our intercessory prayer team. I didn't know what was going on, but I wondered how she was able to be absent without anyone noticing. The pastors weren't scrutinizing, shunning, or rebuking her. Nobody said anything or seemed to care.

When I reached out to her she, said she was fine. No mention of being in trouble with the church. She was busy unpacking her house and the pastors were OK with that. She wasn't in a rush to get things unpacked, either. Months had gone by and she was still at it.

As it turned out, God was using this woman to help me in my process of realizing the oppressive condition I was in. Marsha's husband had been called to military duty in Alaska for two years, which demanded that she and her family leave the church in Colorado Springs. But within two years of the move to Alaska, they petitioned to get re-stationed in Colorado Springs in order to come back to the ministry. Astonishingly, their wish was granted, but when they returned, they attended church once and never returned.

I didn't get it. They'd moved back to Colorado just to reconnect with the church and now they weren't even coming. I kept calling her to ask her to come to our prayer groups, but she would resist and say she was still unpacking her house.

A month went by, then two, and still no sign of her in church. I reached out to her again, and this time she invited me to take the kids for pizza. We talked and laughed like we used to until she mentioned the word *balance* in a conversation about food. At the restaurant I was going to eat a salad and drink some water because of the continual fast I had been on to remain consecrated at all times. Not knowing about my fast, she yelled out to me as I approached the salad bar, "Make sure you eat some pizza and get a cherry Coke while you're at it! You've got to have *balance!*"

The word reverberated in my mind like a soothing melody. It gave me great peace. So I went and got pizza and a cherry Coke, which I hadn't had in at least a couple of years.

With *balance* continuing to flow through my mind, I looked at Marsha. "Can I share something with you?"

"Sure," she said.

The words just came out of my mouth like a gushing geyser. I couldn't believe it. I'd never shared this with anyone. I told her about my financial circumstances and personal things that had happened to my family in the church. I told her that my husband was a contractor in Iraq and that my home was about to be foreclosed on. I told her how my car had been repossessed. I told her I didn't have enough money for gas. I told her there were times when I had no money for groceries or even toilet paper. I told her about the co-signed loan and I told her I was so nervous, intimidated, and shaky that whenever I was heading to church, I would have to pull over to vomit.

The look on her face was indescribable. She was speechless.

"I give all that I have to the church." I said. "Am I in the will of God?"

"No, that's not God's will for you," she said.

She didn't know it, but her words where like a key that unlocked a door that I was stuck behind.

She was shocked, still staring at me wide-eyed. She told me about a vision the Lord had given her and why she no longer attended the church. She said that what the Lord showed her scared her and that she refrained from sharing it with others for the sake of not causing any discord.

She said she'd had a vision her first Sunday back at church, during an altar call. Those who were at the altar looked like dead men walking, like zombies. "The zombies began to cry as if they were crying out to God; however, they were looking to the pastors as their god, waiting for them to come down from the pulpit and touch them. They cried for the pastors' acceptance, approval, and validation. They were not looking to God at all. In fact, He was not even at the altar."

She couldn't shake the vision, so she never went back.

Undeniable Truths

I sought the Lord and prayed, "Lord, have I truly placed them before you?" I wanted to be a part of the church system and had embraced external religion in order to please men. I had marveled at the church mothers, the nurses, the armor bearers, and all the religious faculties of the church, thinking they would bring me closer to God. I had conformed to external religion instead of being transformed to the loving character of Jesus and had gotten so caught up in the religious flow and hype of ministry that I forgot my first love.

Receiving His love, His grace, and His mercy is what He always desired for me, which hasn't been as easy as I thought it would be. I had to choose to receive His grace over my life. I was busy jumping through hoops and doing everything man deemed to be righteous in the eyes of God without simply embracing His love for me, but God never intended for me to become religious in order to please Him. He wanted me to rest in Him, embrace His love, and enjoy my relationship with Him.

I realized that the Lord had given me exactly what I asked for.

I was an extremely insecure person. I desired for those in leadership to see the good in me. I looked for a prophetic word at every chance. I sought man's approval instead of simply being satisfied with God's approval, and I'd forgotten how to enjoy Him in my everyday life. Seeking man's approval brought problems to my relationship with the Lord, and the things of God became more complex and strained. First Samuel addresses how the Israelites cried out for the Lord to give them a king like the other nations had, failing to realize that God was the King and deliverer over their lives. This, in a sense, was my mistake, too.

"So all the elders of Israel gathered together and came to Samuel at Ramah. They said to him, 'You are old, and your sons do not follow your ways; now appoint a king to lead us, such as all the other nations have.' "

"But you have now rejected your God, who saves you out of all your disasters and calamities. And you have said, 'No, appoint a king over us.' So now present yourselves before the Lord by your tribes and clans." (1 Samuel 10:19)

Breaking Free

Although I never had to take dangerous routes to freedom, I did have to take a mental, emotional, and spiritual journey of breaking free. Just like God led Harriet Tubman to freedom from a slave plantation, God led me to freedom from the enslavement of religion. I inquired of the Lord, and he gave me specific instructions as to how I would escape the church and where I would go.

That same night my girls and I went to Marsha's house for prayer. She asked me to tell her husband all the things I had shared with her. I couldn't help feeling like a battered little girl who couldn't discern that Mommy and Daddy were not good to me as I told him everything I had experienced. He looked at me with sorrow in his eyes, as if he were devastated by this.

After being there for a while, I had the feeling that I was being watched. I walked to the living-room window and peeked through the blinds. What I saw startled me. One of the pastors' cars was parked across the street from the house. I was petrified and didn't want to leave the house. So we decided to pray together. Masha and I spent hours on her living-room floor crying and praying for divine intervention for me and for the church as a whole. I began to realize that I was involved in a cult-like structure, being manipulated, controlled, used and abused for the pastors' benefit.

Marsha's husband's phone rang, and it was Pastor George asking if I was at their house. My eyes were full of tears. Everything inside me was weighted down with grief and sorrow because I had to come face-to-face with reality and reality had blindsided me like a sharp knife in my back and I was hemorrhaging on the floor.

Marsha cried for me and with me, telling me that everything would be OK in a while. I stayed there until I regained enough of my composure to go home. I looked out the window and saw that the pastors' car was finally gone and I went home soon after.

During this time, the cloud continued to hover over my head and the sober feeling remained. "Where do I go from here?" I inquired of the Lord, now that my eyes had been opened to the reality of the situation, and I felt Him speak to my spirit, instructing me to leave Colorado Springs.

It was also during this time that I had a dream in which a giant snake chased my two sisters and me. It chased us everywhere we went and seemed to know our exact whereabouts when we tried to hide from it. It made a ticking sound like a clock, which terrified us to no end. We ran into a room and held each other and cried and prayed as we sat in the corner of the room knowing it would find us. We could hear it swiftly slithering through the house. Suddenly, it burst through the door of the room with a vengeance and wrapped its humongous body around the three of us and squeezed tightly. *This is it. This is how we're going to die.* It wrapped itself around the tops of our heads, but then suddenly an angel of the Lord appeared brightly in the room and gently touched the enormous snake with the point of his finger. Poof—the snake vanished and we were free!

I interpreted the dream to mean that God was delivering me from a horrible situation that was squeezing the life out of me. I felt reassured that God was watching over me and all I had to do was follow His directions. I had to leave the church.

I called my husband in Iraq and told him all that I had told Marsha and her husband. He agreed to put in for immediate orders to leave Iraq and come home within the next two weeks. I told him we had to move out of the city to break away from the cult, and he was in agreement.

Oh, the remarkable fear that captivated us both at the thought of leaving. I was afraid of going to hell for breaking covenant with the pastors. I was afraid of not being accepted by another church after this. I was afraid of failing, afraid of slander, afraid of misunderstanding, afraid of character assassination, and I feared that I was going to die—naturally and spiritually.

I didn't know how I was going to tell the pastors—should we just leave abruptly or let them know we were leaving? I pondered this for days. When Sunday morning came around, I debated whether to go to church. If I didn't go, they might detect that something was wrong, especially since they knew that I had been to Marsha's house the other day. They would come to my house again and I would have to face them by myself with the news of our departure. I didn't know how to explain to them the things God was revealing to me and the cloud that had hovered over me for about three weeks.

Although I was being used in ministry, having finally been deemed worthy of the call of God, and things were going great, I couldn't shake the cloud. I simply felt awakened by the Lord. It was as if He'd removed a veil from my eyes and I could see the bondage I had been in. I didn't want to see—I didn't want the confrontation that comes with seeing truth—but God showed me His truth that couldn't be denied. This truth was His unconditional love for me that no man had the reins to.

I sat there biting my nails as the minutes passed by. It was almost service time, and I knew they'd be outraged if I wasn't there. I felt afraid and deceived at the same time. Coming out of the religious mind-set has trials of its own because you're challenged to shift from being justified by the letter of the law to justification by faith in Jesus Christ and shifting from self-condemnation to godly conviction.

As I sat there still debating, the phone rang. It was Marsha. She asked to pray with me over the phone, which helped me to calm down and relax a bit. Then we began to pray over my nerves and for the church, praying for God's will to be done and for justice to be served. At the height of our prayer, my phone beeped with another caller.

It was Pastor George!

I panicked for a moment. My heart skipped a couple of beats and I took the call. "Hello?"

"Where are you?" he asked slowly and sternly.

"At home," I quietly said.

"Why are you at home? You mean to tell me that you chose to stay at home on the day that your mother is speaking?" He meant Dr. Sharon. "Why aren't you here to intercede while your mother is preaching?"

"Umm ... because I decided to stay home today." All I could think about were the many lies he and his wife had told me and their mental and emotional abuse over the past five years. I thought of all the deception I'd been subjected to and the painstaking effort it took to please them. Then, all of a sudden, something came over me. My heart began to race and I stood on my tiptoes. "Repent! Repent! Repent! Repent! Man of God, repent!"

I couldn't believe those words had come out of my mouth, and why was I shouting?

"Who are you talking to?" he slowly replied.

"I'm talking to you ... That's all I've got."

The phone was silent.

"I'm getting off the phone now," I said.

The phone was still silent, and then I heard a sound as if the phone had dropped to the floor. "Hello?" I asked softly. "Hello? ... Hello?"

He didn't say anything. I waited for a moment, and with no further words I hung up the phone.

I couldn't believe what had just happened. I was shaking, in utter shock. I knew that Dr. Sharon was going to come after me now. I started to panic. I picked up the phone and called Marsha back and told her what had happened. She told me not to worry because I'd done the right thing.

But I was worried. I didn't know what to do next. I knew this was not the end. I had just stirred the pot of confrontation. *What if they show up at my door again to ridicule and scold me?* I felt bad, but justified at the same time.

A couple of hours later, one of the pastors' daughters called. I didn't answer. She was usually the messenger for her family, finding out information and then updating the pastors on a person's status. I just let it ring as I gathered my thoughts.

I knew that Dr. Sharon would be next to call. About an hour later, she did.

"Hello," I said.

"How are you?" she said with a cold undertone.

I trembled at the sound of her voice. "I'm fine."

"So, what is going on, dear? Your dad said he spoke to you about something. Is everything OK? What's going on? Is Derek OK?"

I knew that she had already been well-informed about my conversation with Pastor George. She was a wise, cunning woman who was always five steps ahead of me. She spoke as if she were totally clueless, but I knew she wasn't. I was too familiar with her approach of entangling me in a web of confusion. She spoke kindly and calmly whenever anybody attempted to question or confront her, portraying herself as a victim of the other person's frustration. I knew her game and I didn't want to play anymore. As she spoke, I took a deep breath and mustered up the courage to confront her.

"Mom," I said, "you have been lying to us, tricking us, deceiving us, taking advantage of us, robbing us, manipulating us!" I began to cry. "And I am not going to take it anymore. The people in the church have done nothing but worship the ground you walk on, and they love you beyond measure. And you take from them, ridicule them, mistreat them and bash them. You build us up to tear us down for your benefit, and we have become solely dependent on you, but no more! No more of your lies and your deceit."

"Now, Dee, you know that you get like this when Derek leaves for Iraq."

"No!" I said. "This has nothing to do with me and Derek. This has to do with manipulation, control, and deceit, and I will not be under your control anymore!"

She began to explain the situation as if she were completely innocent. I had to put the phone down while she spoke because I could feel her pulling me back into agreement with her. I knew she could trip me up and have me confused by the time she was finished with me. I could have easily lost sight of the truth. This woman knew how to get inside my head.

But I believe that God was in the midst of this conversation, and He gave me the strength to say no to every plot she had for me.

"Derek and I will no longer be attending church services, so please remove my number from your register."

There was silence.

"OK," she said, and with no further words we got off the phone.

I was shocked. All I'd had to do was say no to her and stand firm on the truth and she said OK!

Was this really it? Five years of committing our lives to these people was over?

I couldn't believe it. *Now what do I do?*

My Husband's Return

My husband returned like a knight in shining armor. We discussed the move that we were going to make and gained clarity from the Lord as we talked it through. Derek reminded me that we were still directly depositing a thousand dollars into Pastor George's account every month, and he called Pastor George to recover the deposit that had been made the day before. Pastor George insisted that they meet at the bank.

When Derek returned several hours later, he told me what had happened. When he'd arrived at the bank, Pastor George told him he needed to be paid back for assisting me with groceries. Derek gave him the money he requested, and they sat and talked for the rest of the afternoon about our departure. Pastor George told Derek that he was his spiritual son and was dear to his heart and that I had broken covenant with them. He said Derek needed to make a choice: go with me and break covenant or continue to serve him and leave me.

"I choose my wife," Derek said.

He told me that Dr. Sharon wanted the prayer cloak that she had given me, since I was no longer a daughter. The cloak had been given to me for being involved in her School of the Prophets mentorship class, and I was happy to give it back to her. Its return would be symbolic of having no lingering attachments.

I called my mom in Georgia. "Mom, we're leaving the church, and I wanted you to know just in case something happens to me."

She prayed with me and told me that a couple of weeks earlier, she had lain on top of photos of my sisters and me, travailing in prayer, asking the Lord to deliver us out of bondage. When she told me this, I cried because I realized that her prayers had gone before me.

Could this have been the reason for the cloud and the disoriented feeling I'd had for three weeks?

I apologized for keeping her at a distance and not listening to her guidance.

"It's OK, baby," she said. "As long as you're free."

A couple of days later, Marsha called me and asked me to come over for a minute. I rushed over to see her and tell her and her husband what was happening. I told her we were moving within the next two weeks. She asked if we had enough money and I told her yes. We had about $1,500 to get us there.

"Well, the Lord spoke to me in a dream telling me to give you and your family our income tax refunds to help you leave the city," she said.

She handed me an envelope. I opened it to find a $3,000 check made out to me. I was speechless and overcome with joy. They said that after losing so much, it was my turn to be on the receiving end. I cried and thanked them for all of their support.

I'll be forever grateful to them.

Moving Forward

Derek looked at me. "Well, where do we go from here?"

"Florida," I replied automatically.

"What's in Florida?"

"I don't know. Possibly ministry. I've been thinking about it all night."

"I'd like to go back home and visit family first before we uproot to Florida."

Derek was right; we hadn't seen our family in years, and the girls didn't know their grandparents. So we both agreed that we needed to go back home to Arizona to reunite with our family.

Within a matter of two weeks, we packed up all our belongings. We sold our beds, TVs, dressers, appliances, and everything else we deemed necessary. The rest went to storage at a facility nearby. We had a thirteen-hour drive ahead of us and we didn't want to haul all our belongings with us.

I couldn't believe we were leaving. My heart and soul were still connected to church, and I couldn't see my life without the pastors in it. I loved the pastors deeply, but I knew that my family had suffered great loss and abuse, and I could not let this continue.

I'll never forget the day we left. A tremendous snowstorm hit Colorado Springs, which was odd because there'd been no sign of a storm the day before. But we were determined to proceed forward with caution. When we got on the road, we promised each other not to turn back, no matter what.

Arizona

The drive to Arizona was long and reflective. We examined our lives and what they had come to, realizing that our family had gone through a major crisis that left us financially deprived, physically and spiritually bankrupt, and mentally exhausted. I felt as if my heart had been torn out of my chest, leaving a hole in its place. The reality of our situation hit me over and over again and I silently wept to myself.

Dr. Sharon held the keys to my very existence. What would I do without her? In my heart, I knew my relationship with her had been extremely unhealthy. I'd lived my life on edge and jumped through hoops for acceptance. We put our trust in two people who took over our lives, costing me my career, our home, our vehicles, and our credit scores. We didn't know where we were going to stay or where the next check was coming from. All we knew was that the Lord had told to us to leave the city.

When we arrived in Arizona, our family members joyously celebrated our return. Most of them had no idea of all that we had gone through, since we'd held them at bay over the years. When they heard about the details, they were shocked and disturbed by our losses and the fact that we'd kept them out of the situation.

My sisters hugged me, my dad held me close to him, and my mother relocated from Georgia to Arizona to be by my side. She never said, "I told you so." She comforted me each day as I stumbled with the concept of moving forward. She cried with me, prayed with me, and nurtured me back to stability. I tried to go to church, but it wasn't the same. I was no longer standing and praying with the microphone in my hand. Now I was sitting, trying to pick up the pieces of my devastation. It was as if a tornado had hit, destroying all my belongings, taking all my aspirations, and leaving me deserted. But the fact of the matter was that I still had my right mind, glory be to God. And my daughters never felt the hit we'd taken because they were too young to know what was really going on.

By God's grace, we found a furnished apartment within a week. We moved in on the following Monday and began our new lives. Derek got a job working with troubled youths and I got a job working part time at Sears Holdings. The transition took some getting used to. I didn't know how to live outside the limitations the pastors had set for me, and I still had bouts of anxiety. On the other hand, I felt freer and freer as the days went by. Freedom to just be Dee!

We lived in Arizona for two years, and during those two years God poured his mercy and grace upon us. Everything just seemed to work out for us, and we didn't want for anything. Although we still had the bankruptcy, the car repossession, the co-signed loan, and the home foreclosure to recover from, God showed us that His hand of approval was upon us and He blessed us in every attempt we made to move forward.

Chapter 8

Ownership

Derek and I examined our hearts time and time again, trying to figure out why this devastation had happened. And we decided to take full responsibility for the trials that had come upon us. We'd been deceived, but we also had to admit that we'd put man on a pedestal and that this had opened a door by which the enemy could come into our lives like a flood. I was ignorant of the enemy's schemes and devices. In a spiritual sense, I ran after man and consequently received man's leprosy just as Gehazi ran after Naaman and received his leprosy in 2 Kings 5:26-27.

> "But Elisha said to him, 'Was not my spirit with you when the man got down from his chariot to meet you? Is this the time to take money or to accept clothes—or olive groves and vineyards, or flocks and herds, or male and female slaves? Naaman's leprosy will cling to you and to your descendants forever.' Then Gehazi went from Elisha's presence and his skin was leprous—it had become as white as snow."

Thank God for His grace, because if I'd been Gehazi, I would have been doomed. Truthfully, His heart did go with me, but I didn't trust my God-given instinct and discernment warning my heart not to pursue. I desired for man to say "You are prophetic" or "You are a teacher" or "You are an intercessor (prayer advocate)" instead of waiting for the Lord to tell me who I am through my relationship with Him.

Man's approval required me to jump through hoops, act like somebody else, and exhaust myself with works. I thought I needed to display external religious formalities and the traditions of man in order to please God. I wanted the form of godliness and denied the power thereof. I wanted all that I saw on television, the spiritual hype of it all, without realizing that the Lord was calling me into relationship with Him.

The form of godliness became my cry for a king when I already had access to sit at the feet of the King of Kings and fellowship with him. I got caught up in glorifying the vessels that God uses and lost sight of Jesus, who is the treasure within the earthen vessels. I so admired the gifts of the spirit that they blinded me. I didn't realize that the gifts of God are without repentance. I was easily fooled, thinking that because the anointing was present, surely the church leaders had the right motives in regard to me.

I've since learned that people can operate in gifts and not have the love of Christ in their hearts. This is why the Bible tells us to beware of false prophets and you will know them by their fruit (Matthew 7:15-16), which is godly character. Gifts and the fruit are different. As Galatians 5:22-23 says, "Therefore, don't be easily moved by the gifts, but look for the fruit of the spirit, which is love, joy, peace, longsuffering, gentleness, goodness, faith, meekness, and temperance." Those are the result of God's work in the believer.

> "By their fruit you will recognize them. Do people pick grapes from thorn bushes, or figs from thistles?"
> Matthew 7:16

Restraints of Condemnation

A lot of healing had to take place before I found a healthy balance in my life. Every shortcoming became a justifiable reason to condemn myself. For years, I struggled with going through religious formalities before I could receive God's forgiveness. I worked for Christ's approval through self-deprivation. I became overwhelmed with trying to live a holy lifestyle for Jesus. I burdened myself with multiple tasks at church, and I felt as if I had to pray for hours or fast every other day to be acceptable to God.

I had a robotic system going that deprived me of true relationship with the Father. In my mind, I had to work in order to be deemed righteous, but in actuality, I was seeking God through reason and imagination, preventing myself from resting by the redemption He has given me. This is where I'd fallen into the trap of outward religion, which demands self-effort and works. I knew that His forgiveness was there, but I wouldn't allow myself to receive it. I wondered what was wrong with me, why I felt so burdened.

I couldn't break free from the sorrow and guilt I felt when I made a mistake; it just lingered on and on. It wasn't because I didn't want to let go. I just couldn't. I'd functioned in legalism for so long that I didn't know how to rest and receive His grace. I wanted to be morally perfect in a sense, formulating my own ideology of what God wanted or expected of me.

I was exhausted, feeling defeated, unworthy, and condemned every day, but this time I was condemning myself. Every night I went to bed with thoughts of how I could have done certain things better or how I'd failed God that day. The weight of my sins became extremely heavy.

One Sunday morning after church service, I found a book in the back of the car titled *Resting in His Redemption,* by James P. Gills, M.D. The title of the book penetrated my heart and my eyes filled with tears.

"Where did you get this?" I asked Derek.

Ownership

He told me a friend had given it to him and he tossed it into the back of the truck.

"I need this!"

After reading the book, I realized what I needed to do: completely give myself over to God's divine rest.

I shut out all the negative voices of condemnation and asked the Lord to give me rest. I made a conscious decision to quiet my soul and receive His love, peace, grace, and new mercies every morning. His yoke is easy and His burden is light. I no longer had to prove myself worthy of His love, because He loved me anyway.

> "Come to me, all you who are weary and burdened, and I will give you rest. Take my yoke upon you and learn from me, for I am gentle and humble in heart, and you will find rest for your souls. For my yoke is easy and my burden is light." Matthew 11:28-30

I had to receive the Lord's forgiveness over my life. It was my responsibility to repent for my mistakes and shortcomings and then *move on,* never to stay in a place of defeat again.

It took faith to embrace God's redeeming sacrifice over sin. God delivered me from sin and death when He said, "It is finished," and I believe Him. No longer do I have to carry guilt, condemnation, unworthiness, and hurt.

We were brought with a price—Christ's sacrificial death—and therefore we are free from Satan's deceitful grip.

Chapter 9

Religion

Satan deploys the religious spirit to make it difficult for man to receive God's grace. The spirit comes to set up a false system of order within the church through religious customs, rituals, and formalities, leading man to major in the minor things in the church and distracting him from receiving the Gospel of Jesus Christ.

The religious spirit is on assignment to make it difficult for man to enter into the presence of God by placing perceived limitations on God's grace and mercy over their lives, preventing them from being submerged in Christ's love. A friend of mine once said that religion is like being confined with chains, and I agree. With limited access to the Father's grace, mercy, and love, the confined person can get only so far.

God wants us to have full access to Him. He doesn't mind if we swim in the healing waters of his mercy. He wants us to be restored, healed, and made whole. In John 5:6, Jesus asked the man who'd had an infirmity for thirty years if he wanted to be made whole. He didn't ask if the man wanted only a portion of his grace:

"I command religious chains to be broken off your life in the name of Jesus!"

Religion is not based on love; it is a system of spiritual concepts, practices, rituals, rules, or beliefs that we use as a means to connect to God or be in right standing. What we fail to realize is that in all our doing and in all our knowing, we can become self-righteous if we don't operate in His love and in His character. We invoke a form of godliness but deny the power thereof.

> "But mark this: There will be terrible times in the last days. People will be lovers of themselves, lovers of money, boastful, proud, abusive, disobedient to their parents, ungrateful, unholy, without love, unforgiving, slanderous, without self-control, brutal, not lovers of the good, treacherous, rash, conceited, lovers of pleasure rather than lovers of God—having a form of godliness but denying its power. Have nothing to do with such people.
>
> They are the kind who worm their way into homes and gain control over gullible women, who are loaded down with sins and are swayed by all kinds of evil desires, always learning but never able to come to a knowledge of the truth." (2 Timothy 3:1-7)

The truth is salvation through Jesus Christ! We must continually abandon ourselves to His grace—without working—to receive His grace, love, and peace in our lives. We create our own righteousness and become our own god in a sense when we pile up our works on top of His redemption. All of our righteousness is as filthy rags.

> "All of us have become like one who is unclean, and all our righteous acts are like filthy rags; we all shrivel up like a leaf, and like the wind our sins sweep us away." (Isaiah 64:6)

Perfectionism Goes Hand in Hand With Pride

I have often heard people say, "Oh, I'm a perfectionist. That's why I'm so hard on myself and others." I've said it myself plenty of times. But here's the thing: perfectionism is a form of bondage because it restricts a person from the freedom to make mistakes. Mistakes are orchestrated as God's learning tools. There is something to learn in every mistake. So don't try to restrict yourself from them. I'm not saying to go out and purposefully be foolish but to give yourself room to make mistakes and learn from them.

We are not perfect. Only God is perfect. God has met the standard of perfectionism for us, and thus we are to follow after His ways and allow Him to perfect us day by day. Our own perfection and our own righteousness can generate the works of pride. We become prideful when we think we have reached a level of perfection or believe we have arrived. Satan believed he was equal to God because he was finely constructed. Ezekiel 28:15 and 17 tell us that he was created perfect in all his ways but that iniquity was still found in him:

> "You were blameless in your ways from the day you were created till wickedness was found in you ...
>
> Your heart became proud on account of your beauty and you corrupted your wisdom because of your splendor. So I threw you to the earth; I made a spectacle of you before kings."

God did not put iniquity in Lucifer—He found it in him—and this tells us that Lucifer created iniquity. Lucifer thought more highly of himself then he ought to have. He had corrupted wisdom by reason of his brightness, the Scripture says. This tells us that corrupt wisdom exists and that Satan himself produces it. So don't believe for a second that this wisdom is not in operation in the church.

When we believe we have to have it all together or we can do no wrong, this is a clear sign that pride has reared its ugly head. Some of us strive to be a cut above the rest, and that's OK when our motives are in alignment with the love of Christ. You see, perfection's underlying factor has to do with self-worth, and any time self is involved, you can bet that pride and arrogance lurk nearby. Perfectionism appears to be a strength, but it's not a strength—it's a weakness when we don't rely on Christ. It causes a person to look down on another person in order to feel a sense of self-empowerment, but this show of self-empowerment is actually an attempt to fill a void in self-worth.

> "Pride has lost sight of the gap between the holy Creator and sinful humanity, producing self-absorption and contempt for others."
>
> -Kelly M. Kapic

Perfectionism also leads people to become worried about what others think or feel about them, which becomes the motive or driving force for what perfectionists do. I'm not advising you to be messy or uncaring but simply to enjoy a life of resting in God's grace and His ability to empower you to carry out His will. Pull from the strength of the Lord because in our weakness He is made strong. Embrace the fact that He loves you whether you color inside the lines or outside the lines.

You are special to Him, and He never intended for you to work for His approval. Jesus paid it all, and all our efforts to be righteous can never measure up to God. That's why we are in need of Him. We will never achieve total moral perfection as long as we live on earth. He is perfect; we are not.

The English word *perfect* suggests flawlessness, but the Hebrew and Greek versions of the word refer to the notion of completeness.

The Hebrew word for *perfection* in biblical Scripture is *tamiym*, which means integrity, truth, upright, full, whole, and complete.

It's not within ourselves alone but through Christ that we realize perfection, as Matthew 5:48 says:

"Be ye therefore perfect, even as your Father which is in heaven is perfect."

It is in Him that we live, move, and have our being. When the Bible uses the word *perfect*, it's in the sense of being mature. We are not flawless but we are asking God to lead us and guide us in all ways. Our nature is sinful and we need the Lord to guide us toward maturity. As Romans 8:7 says, "An unregenerate or carnal mind is enmity against God."

You can be a Christian and still have a sinful mind. The sinful mind is hostile to God because it is self-seeking. Yes, even Christians can have hidden motives for righteousness, like the desire for approval, promotion, or elevation. We must enter into a place of wholeness where we can rest in His redemption. When we rest we are yielding to all that He planned for us to do, not seeking someone else's anointing or someone else's identity. I had to allow the Holy Spirit to give me my identity in Him and show me His will for my life.

I spent years trying to figure out my purpose, but I have learned that there is purpose in all that I do and I am not limited to a specific thing. I did not see purpose in being married and having two children. I thought purpose was only to have a gift or a capacity to do something great and I wanted to be great! I wanted to have a fivefold ministry gift (apostle, prophet, evangelist, teacher, and preacher), and I subconsciously neglected the purpose of being a wife and a mother. I didn't physically neglect my family, but I was emotionally tied to the notion of being somebody great for God.

The Lord began to challenge my heart. "What are your motives?" He asked me one day in prayer. "Why do you want to become great in the kingdom?" It was then that I began to examine my heart. Did I really want to do something great for God or did I desire to be great to cover my lack of self-worth? My zeal said yes, I undoubtedly desire to do something great for

God, but when He opened my eyes to see what lay beneath the surface of my zeal, I gasped in utter despair. My motivation had been driven by acceptance, approval, validation, and *self-worth*.

I looked away. "No, Lord, that's not true," I said. "You know I love you. And all I want is to see your will in my life."

"Adhere to the needs of your husband and children," he said gently. "Treat them kindly and love them."

I realize that now my purpose is to be a reflection of Him and that my gifts are not limited to the four walls of the church but stretch far past the building and touch the lives of every person I connect with.

We tend to get stuck in the systematic flow of religious order and forget that it takes relationship with the Father to have balance within our constructive lifestyles and that relationship is what we need in order to flow in His love, grace, and mercy toward one another. His character is continually being developed in us, and in this process of development He will show us how to love his people.

I had an encounter with Jesus Christ, who revealed His love for me regardless of what I believed about myself. I gained a new perspective on Christian living and now devote my heart to resting in His redemptive power. Having an encounter with the Word has affected my life in such a way that I now desire to share the love of Christ without the motive of feeding my self-worth.

> "In your relationships with one another, have the same mindset as Christ Jesus." (Philippians 2:5)

God wants us to have the mind-set of Christ, not self-seeking but humble, so that we can simply embrace a relationship with the Holy Spirit and come to rest in Him. Webster's dictionary defines *rest* as "freedom from activity or labor." When we rest in Him we become free from works, and we can truly embrace who He has called us to be without the weight of feeling like you must do something to gain his approval. Resting in Him means to let go and let God work in your life. He is the author and finisher of our faith; therefore, He will lead us and guide us in all things. He wants us to experience His perfect love that casts out fear—fear of disapproval and condemnation, which are designed to plague and torment. When you embrace His love for you, you will no longer have to jump through hoops seeking validation from man.

Second Corinthians 5:21 tells us that we were reconciled to God through Jesus Christ, as he bore our sins on the cross so that we could become the righteousness of God:

> "God made him who had no sin to be sin for us, so that in him we might become the righteousness of God."

An exchange like no other took place in that very moment. He took on the weight of sin within the world, and we took on the privilege of being called righteous. Having Him in our hearts is having the gift of His righteousness and salvation.

> For it is by grace you have been saved, through faith— and this is not from yourselves, it is the gift of God. (Ephesians 2:8)

Salvation was freely given to us; we cannot work our way into heaven. It was given freely so that no man could boast within himself. I find that there is a fine line between perfection and pride. When we try to be as perfect as God, we can easily fall into pride. We must allow the Holy Spirit to perfect those things that we have no control over and the things we try to make happen on our own. We must give them over to the Lord in prayer and trust that He has our best interests at heart. As Psalm 138:8 says:

> "The Lord will perfect that which concerneth me: thy mercy, O Lord, endureth for ever: forsake not the works of thine own hands."

Religion thrives on perfectionism and this breeds disproportionate self-esteem, enabling a person to become self-righteous. Self-righteousness is a feeling or display of moral superiority derived from a sense that one's beliefs, actions, or affiliations are of greater virtue than those of the average person. When someone thinks more highly of himself than he ought to and works toward greatness within himself, he's being self-righteous.

Generally, we all want to feel important and believe we have some value, and we must yield to the Holy Spirit's guidance along the path of life and allow Him to reveal our purpose in life. He humbles us and shows us who we are in Christ. Without the love of Christ operating in our character, we can become puffed up because of a position or qualification or even because of experiences and encounters we've had with the Lord.

Chapter 10

Relationship

Relationship derives from communication. Communication is an exchange of information between one person and another. For instance, I have to communicate with my spouse in order to know his heart and the things he desires, and vice versa. Communication allows me to gain an understanding of his character, and when I gain an understanding of his character, I have access to his feelings for me as well. Knowing him allows me to know how he operates.

When my husband and I have a misunderstanding or my feelings get hurt, he will often say to me, "Know my heart, Dee. I am not trying to hurt you. Just understand the place that I am coming from." This would help me to stop and think about my husband's normal intentions, and they are never to deliberately hurt me. He is asking me to look a little deeper, not just on the surface of the misunderstanding but to see his intent because I know his feelings about me.

This is similar to knowing the heart of God. God tells us in Jeremiah 29:11 that He has thoughts of peace toward us and not of evil:

"For I know the thoughts that I think toward you, saith the Lord, thoughts of peace, and not of evil, to give you an expected end."

Let me go a little deeper for a moment. When I am having a miscommunication with God because I do not understand what He is doing in my life and why He is allowing certain things to happen, I *must* revert back to knowing His heart based on the relationship we have already established. He doesn't want to kill me. He has the best intentions for my life, and trusting His judgment is everything. If I don't know the heart of God and His intentions for me, I will constantly misunderstand Him.

Daily communication is the key to developing a relationship with the Lord. It is us knowing him and him knowing us. He wants to be a part of our daily lives. He wants us to acknowledge his existence on the earth; He wants us to know how much He loves us. When we rely on ourselves for peace, love, comfort, and joy, we are rejecting God's assistance; we are like children who reject the guidance of their parents.

He wants to hear us say we trust Him and need Him in order to experience, peace, love, comfort, and joy. He wants us to tell Him who hurt us, who made us angry, what we need, what we desire, how we feel. Most of the time, communicating with the Lord will transition into prayer, and prayer simply moves the heart of God. When you are interested in someone or you want to know someone a little better, you communicate with him or her. You spend time with that person, whether you're going to lunch or dinner; you make time for the person you want to know. The Lord is interested in knowing us. Matthew 7:23 comes to mind:

> "Many will say to me on that day, 'Lord, Lord, did we not prophesy in your name and in your name drive out demons and in your name perform many miracles?' Then I will tell them plainly, 'I never knew you. Away from me, you evildoers!'"

This passage of Scripture tells me that people are capable of doing wonderfully great works for the Lord, prophesying and casting out devils, while still not *knowing* the Lord. What is it to know the Lord then? Knowing the Lord is to know love, not only knowing His love for us but also knowing how to love His people. So often we get caught up in being about our Father's business that we forget the love factor of His business.

> "Love is patient, love is kind. It does not envy, it does not boast, it is not proud. It does not dishonor others, it is not self-seeking, it is not easily angered, it keeps no record of wrongs. Love does not delight in evil but rejoices with the truth. It always protects, always trusts, always hopes, always perseveres." (1 Corinthians 13:4-7)

If this is what the Bible says love is and these are the attributes of love, why do we condemn ourselves through religious practices and rituals in an attempt to make God love us or forgive us for our shortcomings? God's love for us surpasses our own comprehension. If our heart condemns us, 1 John 3:20-21 says, then know that God is greater than our heart because He knows all things, and far exceeds the rationale of our hearts. The heart is desperately wicked, above all who can know it. So do not give way to the feelings of condemnation.

Stuck Between Religion and Relationship

- I became stuck when I didn't wait on God to show me my identity in Christ.
- I became stuck when I didn't trust the leading of the Holy Spirit.
- I became stuck when I let man's validation and approval override God's.

- I became stuck when I didn't go back and study the word of God for myself in order to get a clear understanding of the context of Scripture.
- I became stuck when I was desperate to achieve God's purpose for my life without going through the process of growth and maturity.
- I became stuck when I operated out of my own selfish ambition.
- I became stuck when I fell under the pressure of what man required me to be instead of being who God had called me to be.
- I became stuck when I listened to the lies of the enemy that sought to condemn me.

Please learn from my mistakes and wait on God to show you who you are in Christ. Read and study the Bible in order to know the Scriptures and the proper context of Scripture for yourself. Trust the Holy Spirit to lead and guide you in all things. Trust that He has thoughts of peace toward you, and not of evil, to give you an expected end; you don't have to rush and take matters into your own hands. Go through the process of growth and maturity. And most important, while you're waiting on the Lord, love and help others to the best of your ability.

Ministry opportunities are all around us. Your name doesn't have to have glitter and have lights all around it to be noticed by God. You don't have to be connected to a mega-ministry or have a title attached to your name to please Him. Don't yearn to be a big name in the church, but desire that the complete work of Christ be done in your heart and on the earth.

There were times when I wanted to reach my destiny so badly that, without realizing it, I took matters into my own hands and failed to trust the Lord to open doors for me. I was anxious for man to notice that I had a calling in my life, too; therefore, I did everything in my power to be received by man.

For some strange reason, I subconsciously thought that mimicking church leaders' personalities, characteristics, and appearances would bring me closer to God, but in actuality, it took the place of developing my personal relationship with the Lord. Mimicking the authenticity of others hinders us from finding out who we are in Christ.

Be true to you and be yourself. Embrace who you are so you won't seek approval from man. The Lord will use your uniqueness for His purpose. He made you special on purpose. He knew you before your existence on the earth. Ask him what your purpose is and lean on the Holy Spirit to guide you. The Holy Spirit will tell you who you are during those special moments of prayer and fellowship with Him. He will show you your value on the earth.

Before I ever knew how to study the word of God, my relationship with Him had been developing in my prayer time. I'm not saying that studying the word is not beneficial to the development of your relationship with Him, but prayer will ignite the passion to study because it is the Word of God that trains us to know the heart of God and properly interpret life's circumstances. It is the manual for life.

I remember a time when the Lord woke me before dawn just to share His heart with me. I felt Him tug on my heart to arise and commune with Him. So I did.

"Sister James is having her baby this morning," He said to my surprise.

"Really, Lord?" I said, and it was as if I felt Him smile.

Sure enough, Sister James went into labor early that morning and had a beautiful baby girl. I couldn't believe it. I was awestruck! This is the kind of thing He cares about. This is the kind of relationship the Lord desires to have with us. Simple obedience and adherence to the voice of the Lord brings you into divine communion with Him. It is not about rituals, sacrifices, traditions, legalism, or even condemning ourselves before the Lord—it's about simply answering the call to commune with Him. He is loving, He is gentle, and He tugs on our hearts for relationship.

He doesn't force His way in; He knocks at the door and patiently waits for us to open the door.

Holiness

> "Holiness is more than an abstract concept, more than a theory to be proved, more than a doctrine to be dissected. Holiness is a way of living made possible through a personal relationship with God. Life and relationship replace letter and law."
> – Dr. Franklin Moore

Holiness is not an outward appearance or a discipline needed to be learned. It is the developing relationship with the Father. It is the open channel of communication with Jesus and acknowledging Him in our daily lives. To be holy is to simply recognize His love for us and allow Him to develop that same love through us.

I always thought holiness was a way of thinking, speaking, sounding, or dressing, but I was wrong. We truly do not know what holiness is until the Holy Spirit makes it known to us. Holiness is not to be superspiritual, nor is it to be zealous about God. There is a difference between holiness and being superspiritual. Superspiritualism is, in fact, counter to holiness; it is an appearance of godliness that is obtained through self-righteousness, judgment, and supremacy. It is when we become overly cautious about our situations, circumstances, people, and communication to the point where we are not able to relate to others on a natural level. Superspiritualism leads us to hide from our human nature and become intolerant of our flaws and the flaws of others. But we don't hide only from our human nature—we also hide from God instead of allowing him to perfect that which concerns us.

Superspiritualists do everything in their power to live righteously through works, religious concepts, rituals, and customs.

But all the while, God wants us to put on the power of the Holy Spirit to lead us and guide us in all ways so that we don't have to live in a state of being overly cautious about life. Have you ever tried to communicate with someone who is superspiritual? It's almost as if such people are looking at you through a microscope to judge your thoughts and perspectives in order to bring correction to your very nature. They tend to hear out of the place of judgment rather than love.

I once shared with someone that I was experiencing a difficult season in my life, and her response was, "Don't say that it is difficult; God's yoke is easy and His burden is light."

I understood that, but it didn't negate the fact that I was experiencing a difficult season. It's OK to say I'm having a hard time. We are not robots without emotion. God gave us emotions on purpose. Feelings help us to discover ourselves and bring changes in our journey through life and in the lives of others. Expressing that you're having a hard time does not mean you do not trust in God. It simply means you are having a hard time and you need the strength of God to help you through a difficult situation or circumstance. Where we are weak, He is strong. We are supposed to have challenges and call on the Lord for help and strength. In this, His glory is made manifest in us.

Love

"Lord, give me a kingdom mind-set," I said one morning in intense prayer, quoting a phrase I'd heard a preacher once say. It referred to a kingdom outlook on life, with purpose and strategic thinking. I cried out in desperation, feeling as if my purpose in life had been altered because of all that I had gone through.

He answered me with one word: "Love."

This can't be your response, almighty, all-knowing God. I am in a crisis, I have no direction, and you're telling me to love? There's got to be more to it than that. I had just gotten off the roller-coaster ride of religion and didn't know which way to go after spinning out of control.

"I want to see people healed," I said. "I want to see people delivered and set free, and I want to help win souls for you. There is a lot of work in that, so please show me what to do. I have big dreams, God; I have big desires. Give me a kingdom mind-set!"

"Love," He said again in a calm, cool, and collected manner.

I was expecting the Lord to download something big, something huge, into my spirit, the answer to fulfilling purpose and walking in the fullness of all that God had for me to do, but "Love" was all He said. Nothing more and nothing less.

Since then, I have found that love is the key to the heart of God and that doing His will on the earth through love makes a world of a difference when dealing with His people.

Forgiveness

"For God so loved the world that he gave his one and only Son, that whoever believes in him shall not perish but have eternal life."

John 3:16 can be quoted by Christians/non-Christians alike. It's a great Scripture that reflects not only the love of God but also His forgiveness toward all humanity. God's love (agape) is unconditional and is the purest form of love. God "so loved" the world enough—a world that is full of jealousy, envy, pride, and malice—to come and rescue it from the bondage of sin. "Father, forgive them, for they do not know what they are doing," (NIV) Jesus said in Luke 23:24. He had compassion for those who'd hurt Him and asked that they be forgiven for their ignorance. This is astonishing to me. I ask the same thing for those who hurt me. "Forgive them, for they know not what they are doing."

God set the example for us to follow, and the suffering that I've experienced provides me the opportunity to apply Christ's principle and forgive. I forgive the pastors and their family, and

I've accepted the things that happened to my family and me. They had a purpose in my life and have given me the drive to set others free from the same religious mind-set that had entangled me.

I am determined to reveal the love of Christ for all humanity and unveil the grace of God to His people through faith. I desire for people to experience the fullness of salvation and the freedom Christ has given us by way of the cross. My personal experiences have made me stronger and have enabled me to minister to others with grace and compassion. God has redeemed that time and healed and delivered me. I have since moved on with my life, furthered my education in seminary, joined a wonderful church family and begun ministering to women in prison.

I've come to understand that we all fall short of God's glory; none of us are exempt. We all are in need of His love to navigate us through our lives. Some of us allow his love to come in and some of us do not. God desires for us to embrace His love because His love conquers all fear. When we get to the point where we allow His love to be the driving force in our lives, hurt people can truly be healed. I have no regrets about the things I have encountered, and I believe God will get the glory from my story.

References

Black, M., and H. H. Rowley, eds. 2001. *Peake's Commentary on the Bible.* London: Routledge.

Boice, James Montgomery, and Philip Graham Ryken. 2002. *The Doctrines of Grace: Rediscovering the Evangelical Gospel.* Wheaton, IL: Crossway Books.

Gaebelein, Frank E. 1984. *The Expositor's Bible Commentary (volume 9)—John and Acts.* Grand Rapids, Mich.: Zondervan.

Gills, James. 2011. *Resting in His Redemption: The Basis of Prayer and a Christian Life.* Lake Mary, Florida: Charisma House.

Gundry, Robert H. 2003. *A Survey of the New Testament.* 4th ed. Grand Rapids, Mich.: Zondervan.

Hassan, Steven. 1990. *Combatting Cult Mind Control.* Rochester, VT: Park Street Press.

Kapic, Kelly M. 2012. *A Little Book for New Theologians: Why and How to Study Theology.* Downers Grove, IL: IVP Academic.

Lea, Thomas D., and David Alan Black. 2003. *The New Testament: Its Background and Message.* 2nd Ed. Nashville, TN: Broadman and Holman Publishers.

Moore, Frank. 2001. *Breaking Free from Sin's Grip: Holiness Defined for a New Generation.* Kansas City, MO: Beacon Hill Press of Kansas City.

Strong, James. 1991. *The New Strong's Exhaustive Concordance of the Bible: Classic Edition.* Nashville, TN: Thomas Nelson.

Wikipedia, "Self-righteousness," http://en.wikipedia.org/wiki/Self-righteousness (accessed May 28, 2013).

www.ingramcontent.com/pod-product-compliance
Ingram Content Group UK Ltd.
Pitfield, Milton Keynes, MK11 3LW, UK
UKHW041949230426
12048UKWH00008B/223